DECODING DIGITAL DEMOCRACY

Gen AI, Intelligent Automation and the Government

Table of Contents

3

Author's Bio

Sreenath Gurrapu is a recognized thought leader and expert in the field of intelligent automation. With a career spanning over 9 years, he played a pivotal role in shaping the landscape of business transformation through cutting-edge automation technologies.

Having earned Master's Degree in Computer Science from University of Illinois Sreenath Gurrapu's journey into the world of intelligent automation began early in his career when he spearheaded Intelligent Automation projects at Wipro. This marked the beginning of his unwavering passion for harnessing the power of automation to streamline operations, enhance efficiency, and drive innovation.

Throughout his career, Sreenath Gurrapu has demonstrated an exceptional ability to navigate the dynamic intersection of technology and business. He has a track record of successfully architecting and implementing intelligent automation solutions for a diverse range of industries, including [Public Sector/Energy/Finance]. His insights into identifying automation opportunities, selecting appropriate technologies, and designing robust implementation strategies have garnered him a reputation as a trusted advisor among peers and industry professionals.

Sreenath Gurrapu's expertise extends beyond technical proficiency. He is also a prolific speaker and writer, having authored numerous articles, whitepapers that delve into the intricacies of intelligent automation. His ability to distill complex concepts into accessible insights has made him a sought-after presenter at international conferences and webinars.

In addition to his professional accomplishments, Sreenath Gurrapu is committed to fostering knowledge-sharing and collaboration within the automation community. He actively engages in [mentorship initiatives/contributions to open-source projects/participation in industry associations], reflecting his dedication to advancing the field and nurturing the next generation of automation enthusiasts.

As the automation landscape continues to evolve, Sreenath Gurrapu remains at the forefront, exploring emerging technologies, refining best practices, and envisioning new possibilities for intelligent automation. Through his innovative contributions and visionary leadership, he inspires and empowers organizations to harness automation's transformative potential.

Connect with Sreenath Gurrapu on [LinkedIn/Twitter/Website] to stay updated on his latest insights and contributions to the world of intelligent automation.

linkedin.com/in/sgurrapu/

twitter.com/sgurrapu/

Preface

In the intricate tapestry of the modern age, technology weaves a narrative of transformation. Within this narrative lies the heart of our exploration—"Decoding Digital Democracy: Gen AI, Intelligent Automation, and Government." This book serves as both a compass and a key, unlocking the potential of Intelligent Automation (IA) and Generative Artificial Intelligence (Gen AI) within the realm of government.

As we embark on this intellectual journey, the initial chapters illuminate the foundational concepts that underpin IA and Gen AI. These technologies stand as sentinels of change, poised to revolutionize governance in ways once deemed improbable.

The narrative expands to encompass the dynamic landscape of government initiatives, where digital transformation takes center stage. We peer into the motivations propelling this revolution, spotlighting the aspirations that fuel this evolution.

We encounter IA's tangible benefits to government functions emerging from this exploration. Here, we witness the metamorphosis of operations as processes are streamlined, resources are optimized, and a new era of efficiency dawns. Yet, this transformation has its challenges. The following chapters dissect the intricate considerations governments must navigate to embrace IA fully. These hurdles, though daunting, are pathways to progress, demanding strategic foresight and innovation.

Turning our gaze to the realm of Generative AI, the narrative embraces creativity as a driving force for change. We explore its role in redefining public services, engaging citizens, and reshaping the art of problem-solving.

The book is a symphony of practicality and possibility, traversing the intimate interplay of IA and Gen AI across government functions. From decision-making and security management to ethical considerations, legacy systems integration, and real-world case studies—the narrative navigates the transformation spectrum.

As the book nears its conclusion, we peer through the lens of tomorrow. The final chapter paints a portrait of advancement and opportunity, capturing the governance trajectory shaped by IA and Gen AI. It is a glimpse of a digital democracy where technology paves the way for innovation, efficiency, and a new era of governance.

In your engagement with these pages, prepare to embark on a journey that fuses technology and governance. This narrative seeks to decode the intricacies of the digital age and illuminate the path toward a reimagined democracy.

Chapter 1

Introduction to Intelligent Automation (IA) and Generative AI

The combination of Robotic Process Automation (RPA), ChatGPT, and Artificial Intelligence is leading us toward a future where machines can handle repetitive tasks. It is helpful for humans to focus on creative and innovative endeavors that require unique human qualities. We can expect to see even more upgrades with continuous advancements in AI technology.

It is a world of technology transforming how we work and interact. In this digital era, Robotic Process Automation (RPA), ChatGPT, and Artificial Intelligence (AI) are revolutionizing industries across the globe. From streamlining repetitive tasks to enhancing customer experiences, these cutting-edge technologies have become indispensable in today's fast-paced business landscape.

Robotic Process Automation (RPA)

Robotic Process Automation (RPA) has revolutionized how businesses operate by automating repetitive tasks through software robots. These bots mimic human actions, enabling organizations to streamline operations and increase efficiency.

We are thankful for RPA technology as it saves our time and makes your work error-free. One of the prominent advantages of this technology is its ability to integrate into existing systems smoothly. It does complicated coding with effective modifications.

Whether data entry, invoice processing, or customer queries, RPA can handle routine tasks across various industries. By freeing employees from mundane activities, organizations can redirect their focus to more strategic initiatives requiring critical thinking and creativity.

Implementing RPA reduces costs and improves employee satisfaction as they are relieved from monotonous workloads. Furthermore, it enables businesses to optimize resource allocation and enhance customer experiences by delivering faster response times.

As automation continues to evolve, RPA is set to play an even more significant role in transforming business processes across industries. Its potential applications are wide and varied – from finance and healthcare to logistics and manufacturing.

Introduction to Intelligent Automation (IA):

Intelligent Automation (IA) is a cutting-edge technological approach that combines artificial intelligence (AI) and automation to enhance and streamline various business processes. IA leverages the power of AI algorithms, machine learning, robotic process automation (RPA), and other advanced technologies to enable organizations to automate complex tasks and make realistic decisions based on data analysis. This convergence of AI and automation marks a significant advancement in how businesses operate, enabling them to achieve higher efficiency, accuracy, and adaptability levels.

1. **Synergy of AI and Automation:** Intelligent Automation represents the convergence of artificial intelligence and automation technologies. AI

provides the cognitive abilities that enable machines to understand, reason, learn, and make decisions, similar to human intelligence. Automation, on the other hand, involves the execution of predefined tasks without human intervention. IA combines these two elements, allowing AI-driven systems to automate complex tasks, learn from data, and adapt to changing scenarios.

2. **Cognitive Abilities:** IA systems possess cognitive capabilities such as Natural Language Processing (NLP) and Image Recognition. Natural Language Processing (NLP) allows machines to comprehend and handle human language, thereby aiding human-system communication. Natural Language Processing (NLP) will enable devices to learn and manage human language, helping in human-system touch. Image recognition allows engines to interpret and understand visual content, which is particularly valuable in healthcare (interpreting medical images) and manufacturing (detecting product defects).

3. **Robotic Process Automation (RPA):** Robotic Process Automation is a core component of IA. RPA involves using software robots (bots) to perform repetitive, rule-based tasks that humans would

otherwise do. These bots can navigate through different applications, input data, extract information, and perform actions, thereby reducing errors, enhancing speed, and freeing up human employees for more strategic tasks.

4. **Machine Learning and Predictive Analytics:** IA utilizes machine learning algorithms to analyze large datasets and extract valuable insights. Machine learning enables systems to identify patterns, correlations, and trends within the data. This information can be used for predictive analytics, where IA systems forecast future outcomes based on historical data. As the system continuously learns from new data, its predictions become increasingly accurate.

5. **Adaptive Decision-Making:** IA systems excel at making decisions based on data analysis and predefined criteria. However, what sets them apart is their ability to adapt their decision-making processes in response to changing circumstances. These systems can adjust their actions and decisions dynamically, ensuring optimal outcomes even in uncertain or evolving environments.

6. **Enhanced Customer Experience:** IA improves customer experience through various channels. AI-driven chatbots and virtual assistants offer real-time customer support, answering queries, guiding users through processes, and making product recommendations based on user preferences and behavior. This level of personalization enhances customer engagement and satisfaction.

7. **Data-Driven Insights:** Artificial intelligence systems are adept at analyzing data and extracting insights that may have been overlooked through manual processing. By exploring vast datasets, IA identifies trends, anomalies, and correlations, enabling organizations to make data-driven decisions that lead to operational efficiency and competitive advantage.

8. **Workforce Augmentation:** Unlike the fear of job displacement, IA often aims to complement and enhance human capabilities. By automating repetitive and mundane tasks, IA frees human employees to focus on higher-value activities requiring creativity, critical thinking, and problem-solving skills. Having an engaged and productive workforce is a direct result of this.

9. **Scalability and Consistency:** IA offers the advantage of scalability without sacrificing consistency. Unlike humans, IA systems do not experience fatigue, ensuring that processes are executed accurately and uniformly regardless of the volume of work.

10. **Risk Reduction and Compliance:** IA systems can help organizations adhere to regulations and compliance standards by consistently following predefined rules and procedures. Any deviations or anomalies can be quickly identified and flagged for review, reducing non-compliance risk.

11. **Continuous Improvement:** IA systems incorporate a feedback loop through machine learning. They learn from outcomes as they process data and perform tasks, enabling continuous improvement. This iterative learning process helps organizations optimize processes, enhance efficiency, and adapt to changing conditions.

12. **Challenges and Considerations:** Implementing IA requires addressing challenges such as data security, privacy concerns, ethical considerations (e.g., bias in AI algorithms), change management, and the

potential impact on the workforce. Balancing automation and human intervention is essential to achieve the best results.

Intelligent Automation represents a transformational approach that combines AI's cognitive capabilities with automation's efficiency. It enables organizations to innovate, optimize operations, and stay competitive in an ever-evolving technological landscape. The successful deployment of IA requires a strategic approach considering technology, processes, and human collaboration.

AI and RPA Integration

AI and RPA integration represents a powerful synergy that can revolutionize business processes and decision-making. RPA excels at automating repetitive, rule-based tasks, while AI brings cognitive capabilities and intelligent decision-making.

By combining the two, organizations can achieve greater efficiency, accuracy, and scalability in their operations. For instance, AI can analyze massive amounts of unstructured data, enabling RPA bots to make more informed decisions and adapt to dynamic scenarios.

AI-powered natural language processing (NLP) can enhance the interaction between RPA bots and users, facilitating more human-like conversations and improving user experience. Its integration streamlines processes and empowers businesses to unlock valuable insights from data, optimize resource allocation, and drive innovation.

Implementing AI and RPA integration with caution is crucial. It adheres to ethical guidelines and ensures that the technology remains transparent. It is secure to reap the full benefits of this transformative collaboration.

Understanding ChatGPT

ChatGPT is an exciting development in the world of artificial intelligence. It stands for Generative Pre-trained Transformer, a language model that can generate human-like text responses based on input prompts. This remarkable technology has been trained on massive amounts of internet data. It allows us to understand and mimic human conversation.

One key feature of ChatGPT is its ability to engage in context-rich dialogues with users. Unlike traditional chatbots that rely on predefined rules or scripts, ChatGPT can generate dynamic responses by analyzing the conversation history and using that information to provide relevant answers.

Additionally, ChatGPT has demonstrated impressive capabilities in understanding and responding to various topics. Whether you're discussing current events, asking for advice, or simply engaging in small talk, ChatGPT can adapt its responses accordingly.

It's important to note that while ChatGPT is quite advanced, it may sometimes produce incorrect or nonsensical answers. It relies heavily on statistical patterns rather than proper understanding. OpenAI continues to work towards improving these limitations through ongoing research and iterations.

Understanding how ChatGPT works provides valuable insights into AI-driven conversational agents' potential power and limitations. With further advancements in AI technology like this, we can expect even more upgrade interactions between humans and machines.

Artificial Intelligence (AI) Introduction

AI is the short form of Artificial intelligence. It is a cutting-edge technology that aims to replicate human intelligence in machines. It involves the development of computer systems and the ability to perform diverse tasks that require human intelligence. AI has gained immense popularity and is revolutionizing various industries.

AI computers can train to learn from experience, adapt to new information, and perform complex tasks with minimal human intervention. This technology enables machines to understand natural language. It recognizes speech and images, makes decisions based on data analysis, and even engages in intelligent conversations.

One key aspect of AI is machine learning – a subset of AI. The algorithms enable computers to improve performance 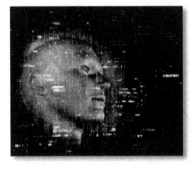 through continuous learning without being explicitly programmed. Deep learning is a fantastic form of machine learning that has played a crucial role in achieving significant advancements in natural language processing and image recognition.

Another vital area within AI is cognitive computing, which focuses on developing systems that simulate human thought processes such as perception, decision-making, and problem-solving. These cognitive systems aim to enhance productivity by augmenting human capabilities rather than replacing them.

The applications of AI are vast and diverse. The possibilities seem endless, from virtual personal assistants like Siri and Alexa to self-driving cars, chatbots for customer service interactions, and fraud detection algorithms in finance systems. Many industries are leveraging the power of AI to streamline operations, improve efficiency, enhance customer experiences, and drive innovation.

AI also poses ethical challenges, such as privacy concerns associated with data collection and usage. As this field evolves rapidly, society must ensure responsible development, guided by ethics, policies, and regulations, to harness its potential benefits while mitigating risks.

Its introduction brings excitement about its potential benefits and cautionary considerations regarding its impact.

We are witnessing an era where humans collaborate more closely than ever with intelligent machines.

AI undoubtedly marks a paradigm shift, redefining what is possible and revolutionizing how we live, work, and interact.

Various Forms of AI

Artificial Intelligence (AI) is a vast field encompassing diverse forms and applications. AI has revolutionized industries and everyday life, from machine learning to natural language processing. Some various forms are mentioned below.

Machine Learning: This form of AI involves training computer systems to learn from data without explicit programming instructions. Machine learning algorithms can make predictions or take actions based on past experiences by analyzing patterns in large datasets.

Natural Language Processing (NLP): NLP enables computers to understand and interact with human language. It encompasses tasks like sentiment analysis, speech recognition, and language translation. With advancements in NLP, virtual assistants like Siri and Alexa have become a primary part of our lives.

Computer Vision: Computer vision allows machines to interpret visual information from images or videos. There are various applications for technologies such as object detection, image classification, and facial recognition. These can be used in multiple fields, from autonomous vehicles to medical imaging diagnostics.

Expert Systems: Expert systems mimic human expertise in specific domains by using knowledge-based rules or decision trees. These systems can provide solutions or recommendations for complex problems based on predefined rules.

Robotics: Robotics combines physical hardware with AI capabilities to perform tasks autonomously or alongside humans. Robots enhance efficiency and accuracy across industries, from manufacturing assembly lines to surgical procedures.

Reinforcement Learning: Reinforcement learning involves training agents through trial-and-error interactions with their environment. It is commonly used in gaming scenarios where an agent learns optimal strategies by receiving rewards or punishments for its actions.

These are just a few examples of the many forms of AI that exist today. With the rapid progress of technology, we can anticipate the emergence of even more innovative applications from this exciting field.

AI Applications and Impact

Artificial Intelligence (AI) has revolutionized multiple industries with its wide range of applications. AI transforms how we live and work, from healthcare to finance, transportation to retail.

One of the most notable applications of AI is in healthcare. With the ability to analyze large amounts of patient data, AI algorithms can help diagnose diseases more accurately and recommend personalized treatment plans. It not only 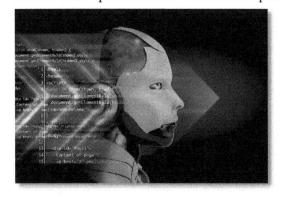 improves patient outcomes but also reduces medical errors.

In the financial sector, AI-powered algorithms can analyze market trends and predict investment opportunities with a higher degree of accuracy. It helps traders make informed decisions and maximize their returns on investments.

Another area where AI is making significant strides is transportation. Self-driving cars powered by AI technology have the potential to overcome accidents caused by human error and improve overall road safety. Also, logistics companies use AI systems to optimize routes for efficient delivery operations.

Retailers leverage AI to enhance customer experiences through personalized recommendations based on previous buying and browsing behavior. Chatbots powered by natural language processing allows customers to interact with businesses 24/7, providing support and answering queries promptly.

The impact of artificial intelligence extends beyond specific industries. It affects society as automation becomes more prevalent through technologies like Robotic Process Automation (RPA). These once manual or time-consuming tasks can be completed rapidly and more efficiently by machines. It frees up human workers' time for more complex problem-solving tasks that require creativity and critical thinking skills.

Concerns about job displacement are due to increased automation driven by AI technologies. While some jobs may be replaced or transformed, new opportunities will emerge— jobs focused on developing, maintaining, and enhancing these intelligent systems.

Generative AI

Generative AI is a thrilling and novel field in Artificial Intelligence and Machine Learning. It uses highly advanced automated tools to create intricate data models and algorithms that can be utilized to automate numerous tasks, thereby cutting down the time spent performing manual labor. Generative AI could have multiple applications across various industries, from forecasting customer preferences to natural language processing. This technology has become one of the most sought-after among entrepreneurs searching for ways to streamline their operations due to its potential usage - which explains why it's quickly gaining popularity.

Understanding the Concept of Generative AI

Generative Artificial Intelligence is becoming increasingly popular these days. It's an evolved form of machine learning in which algorithms produce new information based on what already exists rather than merely processing the data we already have. This approach allows AI to develop fresh and innovative ideas from existing sources and identify patterns within it all - something that would be difficult for a human alone. What kind of insights can this technology uncover?

Generative Artificial Intelligence collects and analyzes vast amounts of data from sources like images, text documents, audio recordings, or videos. Running this dataset through the algorithm can create new outcomes based on what was already present in that initial lot. It will look for patterns and shared similarities between different inputs and then output something innovative off those connections - sometimes even coming up with solutions that wouldn't be conceivable without using traditional methods too and pushing our collective intelligence to its limits.

Generative AI is becoming more and more popular for many tasks. It can predict future events or behaviors, create unique content like music or art, make decisions about items/services, and much more. As its potential continues to grow yearly, many businesses are looking into how they might incorporate generative AI within their company to gain an edge over competitors who have yet to realize the considerable value it offers them. Research whether Generative Artificial Intelligence could benefit your operations now to ensure your business can take advantage of this opportunity. What would that look like? How could it enhance performance compared with what's currently going on?

Generative AI future

Recently, Generative AI (or Artificial Intelligence) has received much consideration in various areas of science and technology. This form of AI is tightly connected to machine learning, and it's utilized for producing novel wares or services. For instance, generative AI may be deployed to devise an original kind of robotics or computer system that can acquire enlightenment from its environment and adjust to specific objectives.

Generative AI also contains enormous potential to bring about paradigm shifts across many industries, including healthcare, agriculture, finance, sector, and transportation, too - not forgetting education. Its impact could be immense if entirely appropriately exploited by the relevant stakeholders.

Generative AI's potential is unique - it can automate complicated processes that would otherwise take humans an enormous amount of time and hard work. If used correctly, this could significantly reduce labor costs while boosting productivity in certain areas. Additionally, these models can develop creative ideas that may not have occurred naturally without their influence – talking about innovation.

What makes things even more exciting is that today we are researching deeper into generative AI every single day. Along with all those advantages, some risks can be associated, too, such as security concerns due to malicious use or data privacy problems if implemented incorrectly within any organization's system architecture. But despite these issues being taken care of appropriately for a successful implementation, one cannot ignore how incredible this technology is – from reducing expenses and providing quality outcomes at blazing speeds never seen before in history; I'm pretty fascinated by what lies ahead in our near future when harnessing advances made towards generative AI.

Generative AI use cases

Generative Artificial Intelligence (AI) is a fantastic new technology that can revolutionize numerous industries. It utilizes deep learning algorithms to generate fresh data from existing datasets, enabling corporations to develop distinct, tailored products or services without needing them to be made manually starting at zero every time. Generative AI can facilitate in many areas, for instance, creating customized content for customers, generating realistic images and videos, and predicting customer needs and habits. This capacity of generative AI is beneficial for businesses within the financial sector since they need quick decisions based on a large amount of information available all over the globe; such capabilities boost their productivity & efficiency drastically.

Generative AI can be used for multiple purposes, like predicting stock market trends or spotting potential investing opportunities. Furthermore, banks could benefit from this technology to gain insights into customer behavior which would otherwise not be accessible, and use it in their marketing plans as well as improve customer service experiences. With generative AI technology, financial organizations can utilize the full range of information available when making decisions related to clientele. Aside from the finance sphere, a broad scope of applications uses generative AI – ranging from other industries worldwide.

Generative AI is a helpful tool that can be applied to various industries. For example, it can be implemented in healthcare systems for diagnosing diseases and developing treatments tailored specifically for each person based on their data - age, gender, health history, etc. Similarly, generative AI also works well with e-commerce platforms where the algorithm-generated recommendations are crafted according to individual user preferences, which gives customers an improved experience - thereby increasing conversion rates. For companies who want to make full use of this technology, however, they must first ensure that their datasets have been appropriately curated; otherwise, accurate predictions from the system cannot be made. Transfer learning is another advanced method worth looking into. It involves training one data set and then fine-tuning its accuracy using another dataset, giving businesses greater flexibility when dealing with different information groups. Lastly, companies should create strategies for implementing this tech within their operations to reap all possible benefits.

Generative AI impact

Generative AI has been becoming increasingly popular in recent years, and its capacity to revolutionize the way we do business and interact with technology is increasingly apparent. This type of AI relies on algorithms that can create new data based on existing facts – a process much quicker than manually creating or gathering data since it eliminates our need for direct involvement. Moreover, this system allows us greater accuracy when predicting results due to its ability to identify patterns present within large data sets quickly. These features make this form of Artificial Intelligence a potent tool that offers fantastic business opportunities in other areas, too - but at what cost?

Generative AI systems are employed by several industries, from finance and the public sector to manufacturing and retail. In finance, generative AI is used to identify trends in stock prices or customer spending behavior, which can help businesses make wise decisions regarding investments or advertising schemes. Healthcare also uses artificial intelligence; it enables medical professionals to evaluate an individual's past health data and symptoms along with doctors' notes - all this information then helps create customized treatment plans catered to each person's particular requirements. What should those suffering from conditions do? How helpful could these new technologies be?

Generative AI quickly becomes essential in manufacturing, retail, and many other industries. With its help, companies can optimize their production processes to minimize energy consumption and materials costs and make more accurate predictions regarding customer behavior that they might have missed out on. What's even better, this technology will only become stronger with time thanks to increasing computing power every year. Organizations can now discover new paths leading them toward the success they may never have considered - all through generative AI systems.

Conclusion

In conclusion, integrating AI and RPA holds immense potential to revolutionize business automation and decision-making. Organizations can achieve unprecedented productivity, accuracy, and adaptability by combining RPA's efficiency in automating repetitive tasks with AI's cognitive abilities.

This fusion allows for better data analysis, natural language interactions, and improved user experiences. However, ethical considerations must be prioritized while embracing this transformative collaboration to ensure transparency, security, and responsible AI usage. As AI and RPA evolve, their seamless integration promises to drive innovation, optimize processes, and create a future where intelligent automation plays a pivotal role in shaping industries and enhancing human capabilities.

Chapter 2

Government Initiatives for Digital Transformation

Ne are living in the ever-evolving landscape of the 21st century. These digital technologies have become instrumental in reshaping economies, societies, and governance. Governments are realizing the importance of utilizing digital technologies globally. Governments are using these tools to improve service delivery, streamline processes, and encourage innovation within public administration.

Digital transformation in the public sector encompasses many initiatives to leverage technology to enhance citizen engagement, streamline operations, and ensure data-driven decision-making.

My dear readers. We will explore the pivotal role of government efforts in adopting digital technologies. It focuses on the importance of Robotic Process Automation (RPA) and Artificial Intelligence (AI) in optimizing government operations. We'll explore various governments' successful digital transformation projects, showcasing exemplary innovation and efficiency enhancement.

Through this exploration, we aim to shed light on the growing significance of digital transformation in the public sector and its potential to shape a more connected, efficient, and citizen-centric governance paradigm.

Definition of Digital Transformation in Government

The government sector's digital transformation involves incorporating digital technologies strategically to improve the delivery of public services. It entails leveraging data analytics, cloud computing, AI, RPA, and more to enhance operational efficiency, transparency, and citizen engagement.

At its core, digital transformation aims to modernize government processes by replacing manual tasks with automated systems that streamline workflows and eliminate redundancies. It enables governments to collect vast amounts of data for analysis and informed decision-making.

Governments can improve their service delivery models by adopting digital technologies. It makes it easier for citizens to access information online without navigating bureaucracies or waiting in long queues for assistance. It is now possible to complete tasks like tax filings, license renewals, and accessing official documents with ease from the comfort of your own home. All it takes is a few clicks.

Moreover, digital transformation empowers citizens by giving them a voice in policy-making through social media platforms or online surveys. Governments can gather valuable insights into public sentiment on various issues and design policies accordingly.

Digital transformation in the government sector is all about harnessing technology's power to create efficient systems that provide seamless experiences for citizens while enhancing transparency within governance itself. The journey towards this tech-driven future holds immense potential for reshaping how governments serve their constituents – breaking barriers between officials and individuals alike.

Importance of Adopting Digital Technologies in the Public Sector

The public sector is vital in our society, providing essential services and governing the nation. However, it is often associated with bureaucracy and inefficiency. In today's rapidly advancing digital age, adopting digital technologies has become imperative for the public sector to streamline processes, improve service delivery, and enhance citizen engagement.

By embracing digital transformation, governments can automate manual tasks, reduce paperwork, and eliminate redundant processes. It not only saves time but also reduces costs significantly. Using digital technologies like cloud computing and data analytics empowers government agencies to manage vast data while ensuring its security efficiently.

Moreover, adopting digital technologies enables governments to provide seamless online services to citizens. From applying for permits to paying taxes or accessing healthcare facilities digitally – these advancements make interactions between citizens and the government more convenient and efficient.

Digital transformation in the public sector also promotes transparency by making information readily accessible to the public. Through open data initiatives and online portals, citizens can easily access government policies, budgets, and performance reports - fostering trust between the government and its people.

Additionally, digital technologies enable governments to collect real-time data on various aspects like traffic patterns or environmental conditions.

These valuable insights help policymakers make informed decisions that benefit both individuals community at large.

Adopting digital technologies is vital for the public sector as it ensures efficiency, cost savings, transparency, and improved citizen services.

Through this continuous innovation, governments are better equipped to meet the time-changing needs of their constituents while ushering in an era of higher productivity, effectiveness, and accountability.

Government Efforts to Adopt Digital Technologies

Governments must keep up with the digital revolution in today's fast-paced and technology-driven world. Integrating digital technologies into the public sector not only boosts productivity and openness but also elevates the level of satisfaction for citizens.

Governments around the world have been taking steps towards embracing digital transformation. They are investing in upgrading their IT infrastructure, implementing e-governance systems, and promoting online services. This shift towards digitization aims to streamline government operations and make them more accessible to citizens.

One such initiative is the creation of government portals where citizens can access various services online, such as applying for licenses or permits, paying taxes, or even registering a birth or marriage. These portals simplify processes that were once time-consuming and cumbersome.

Additionally, governments are leveraging social media platforms to engage with citizens and provide real-time updates on policies, events, or emergencies. This direct communication channel helps bridge the gap between citizens and policymakers.

Furthermore, many governments are investing in data analytics capabilities to gain insights into citizen behavior patterns and preferences. By analyzing this data intelligently, they can make informed decisions that benefit citizens and the government.

These efforts by governments worldwide show a solid commitment to embracing digital technologies. However, there is still much work regarding cybersecurity measures and ensuring equal access for all citizens across different demographics.

The journey towards complete digital transformation may take time but will undoubtedly result in more efficient governance structures that cater to the needs of modern society.

Role of Robotic Process Automation (RPA) and Artificial Intelligence (AI) in Government Operations

The operations of governments are being revolutionized by (RPA) and (AI). With RPA, software robots automate repetitive tasks, while AI enables machines to simulate human intelligence. The combination of these technologies offers great potential for streamlining government operations.

One area where RPA and AI play a significant role is in citizen services. Government agencies can save valuable resources and focus on activities that benefit citizens by automating tedious tasks like data entry and document processing. It leads to improved service delivery and enhanced citizen satisfaction.

RPA and AI can help governments make logical and accurate decisions by analyzing vast amounts of data quickly and accurately. For example, AI-powered predictive analytics can identify patterns. These trends revolutionize public health data to anticipate disease outbreaks or allocate healthcare resources more efficiently.

These technologies enable governments to enhance cybersecurity measures. They can increase the volume of digital threats government agencies face today. RPA tools can proactively monitor networks for vulnerabilities. At the same time, AI algorithms can detect potential cyber-attacks in real time.

RPA and AI have proven their worth during times of crisis management. AI-powered chatbots have been utilized on government websites and social media platforms. It offers immediate information regarding emergencies like pandemics and natural disasters.

By adopting RPA and AI technologies in their operations, governments increase efficiency and pave the way for innovative solutions that address society's complex challenges. The transformative power of these technologies must be considered when creating a more agile and responsive public sector. It caters effectively to its citizens' needs without compromising security or accuracy.

Understanding RPA and AI in the Government Context

Robotic Process Automation (RPA) and Artificial Intelligence (AI) are revolutionizing governments' operations. Software robots are utilized in RPA to automate repetitive tasks, while AI empowers machines to perform intelligent functions that imitate human intelligence. In the government context, these technologies have immense potential to streamline processes, improve efficiency, and enhance citizen services.

RPA can be applied in various areas, such as data entry, document processing, and customer support. By automating these mundane tasks, government servants can focus on more complex and strategic activities. For example, errors can be minimized or eliminated with RPA for data entry processes.

AI can analyze large volumes of data quickly and accurately. It allows governments to gain valuable insights from various sources like social media feeds or public records. Policymakers can make informed decisions based on real-time analytics.

Incorporating AI-powered chatbots into government websites or mobile apps is crucial. It provides citizens with effortless access to information and aid anytime without human intervention. It enhances service delivery and improves citizen satisfaction by providing instant responses.

To improve internal operations and citizen services, RPA and AI adoption in the public sector also contribute towards a more transparent governance system. These technologies provide an audit trail of activities performed by software robots or AI algorithms, ensuring accountability.

However, governments must address privacy and security concerns when implementing RPA and AI solutions. Safeguarding sensitive citizen data should always remain a top priority.

Understanding how RPA and AI fit into the government context makes it clear that their adoption brings numerous benefits, such as increased efficiency, improved decision-making, enhanced citizen services, and greater transparency.

Governments must embrace these digital transformation initiatives to stay ahead in today's rapidly evolving technological landscape.

Benefits of RPA and AI Adoption in the Public Sector

The government's adoption of digital technologies is crucial for driving efficiency, transparency, and innovation in public sector operations. The efforts made by governments worldwide to embrace digital transformation are commendable. Governments can streamline processes, improve decision-making, and enhance citizen services by leveraging technologies like Robotic Process Automation (RPA) and Artificial Intelligence (AI).

The adoption of RPA in government operations brings several benefits. It reduces the chance of human error, allowing employees to work on strategic activities that add value. RPA also helps cut costs by optimizing resource allocation and improving productivity.

AI has immense potential to revolutionize how governments operate. With its capacity to analyze vast amounts of data quickly and accurately, AI can support policy-making decisions based on evidence-based insights. Personalized experiences and automated customer service systems can also enhance citizen engagement.

RPA and AI adoption in the public sector can improve security measures with advanced threat detection capabilities. Governments can leverage these technologies to protect sensitive information from cyber threats effectively.

Embracing digital transformation through the integration of RPA and AI presents a multitude of opportunities for governments worldwide. As technology evolves rapidly, governments must remain agile in adopting innovative solutions that will drive progress across various sectors.

Potential Risks and Mitigation Strategies

Regarding government digital transformation, potential risks must be carefully considered and mitigated. One of the main concerns is data security and privacy. With increasing personal information being collected and stored digitally, governments must prioritize robust cybersecurity measures to safeguard sensitive data from unauthorized access or breaches.

Another risk is the possibility of technological failures or glitches. In any digital transformation project, there is always a chance of technical issues arising, which can disrupt services and erode public trust. To mitigate this risk, governments should invest in regular system maintenance, updates, and thorough testing before implementation.

Resistance to change can pose a challenge during digital transformation initiatives. Citizens may resist adopting new technologies due to unfamiliarity or concerns over job displacement. Governments should proactively address these concerns by providing training programs and support for citizens transitioning into the digital realm.

Financial constraints can hinder the success of government-led digital transformations. Investments in infrastructure upgrades and technology implementation require significant funding. Mitigation strategies include exploring public-private partnerships or seeking external funding sources such as grants or loans.

To ensure successful digital transformations while mitigating risks effectively, governments must take a proactive approach by prioritizing data security measures, addressing technological challenges promptly, addressing citizen resistance through education and support programs, and finding innovative ways to secure the necessary funding.

Successful Government Digital Transformation Projects in the USA

The U.S. certainly has a knack for digital transformation. From government agencies to corporations, digitizing processes fundamentally altered the way we do business and interact with one another. The American government is no exception. It's implemented several successful projects in recent years that have already impacted our lives today.

U.S. Digital Service (USDS)

Have you ever wondered how the government can be efficient and responsive to citizens? The United States Digital Service (USDS) is here to answer that question. This federal agency, launched in 2014 by President Obama, works closely with the executive branch of the U.S.

Government, aiming to improve digital services for citizens, businesses, and other agencies across multiple departments.

USDS focuses on projects such as designing accessible websites and mobile apps and improving data security measures- all these initiatives are geared towards modernizing government operations, making them more efficient, and delivering superior customer service.

By taking advantage of design principles that focus on user needs, such as user-centered design, agile development practices, and technologies like artificial intelligence (A.I.) and machine learning (ML), USDS has achieved numerous digital transformation projects across America. What's more impressive is the ability to leverage these cutting-edge tools to create value for their clients – this indicates an apparent dedication from USDS towards providing best-in-class services. How have they been able to integrate A.I. into their processes so seamlessly? And why should other businesses take note?

The USDS has shown that technology can be used to create better experiences for citizens. Their success stories explain how government agencies use tech effectively and efficiently, reducing waste while increasing access to services or products and focusing on users' needs first.

AI/ML and UX/UI design principles such as usability testing and prototyping iterations have allowed the USDS team to develop digital service transformations which make life easier overall – from creating an online platform for veterans' health care information, managing federal student loan repayment programs in an open source software system, introducing new tools for public transit ridership tracking across several states along with improved online voting systems.

Federal Risk and Authorization Management Program (FedRAMP):

FedRAMP is a government-wide program established in 2012 as the U.S. Homeland Security Department of and General Services Administration initiative. It's meant to provide a standardized approach for assessing, approving, and carefully monitoring cloud products and services used by federal agencies. This platform aims to make digital transformation projects within the USA successful – how's it done? Well, through providing authorized access to all Cloud-related solutions available.

Using FedRAMP, agencies can ensure their users are accessing only secure systems they have been authorized for. It reduces the risk of data breaches and cyber security threats against government departments. The program was made to allow organizations to stick to rigorous safety requirements while making it easier for new systems to join their infrastructure network.

FedRAMP requires companies to give out paperwork outlining what kind of system design they use, test results within those designs, maintenance processes in place, and incident response plans before authorization is granted or approved by an independent third-party assessor who reviews everything thoroughly beforehand.

Ensuring all necessary components are digital before government departments use them helps reduce risks associated with improper system design or implementation. Furthermore, FedRAMP provides a consistent security approach across various federal agencies and a bonus of cost-saving advantages for vendors. For example, if they've achieved certification from one agency, those same certifications could be used when requesting bids from other governmental bodies, thereby eliminating the need to undergo expensive assessments each time they bid on new contracts - making it more viable for companies such as construction firms and I.T. businesses, etc., to do business with the government without breaking their budget which would otherwise make them less competitive in some instances.

NASA's Open Data Initiative

The United States government has significantly succeeded with its digital transformation project, the NASA Open Data Initiative. This initiative was launched in 2015, and its primary goal is to make all of NASA's research and data available for public use. Through this program, they aim to increase transparency and reduce costs while allowing scientists worldwide to work together more efficiently. With over 200 publicly accessible datasets made possible by projects like Cassini-Huygens or Hubble Space Telescope - name two - and Mars Rover Curiosity, everybody can now access NASA's stored information at no cost – quite impressive.

Apart from granting access to these datasets, NASA is also providing tutorials for those individuals that require assistance on how best to utilize them. It ensures researchers have the tools to work within this open data sphere effectively. The Open Data Initiative has significantly affected scientific exploration, allowing people everywhere to join forces and exchange knowledge without having to be in the same place or organization.

This project has proven to be a success for many organizations across the U.S., such as Harvard Business

School, awarding it their 2019 Digital Transformation Award. It recognizes its role in helping scientific discovery while promoting open-source development practices worldwide. Unsurprisingly, President Obama signed an executive order in 2016 supporting federal agencies participating in similar initiatives from NASA and other departments.

Some more examples are below.

1. **Contract Modification Automation:** In 2020, the IRS's procurement division faced the challenge of modifying 1,500 contract clauses to comply with changes in federal legislation. Using RPA, the procurement team could execute these modifications within 72 hours, a process that would have taken a year to complete manually. This automation reduced administrative burden, eliminated data errors, sent modification emails to vendors, and uploaded documentation into the contract repository.

2. **Data Formatting and Consolidation:** The IRS plans to utilize RPA bots to format data and consolidate information from multiple data sources. This task involves extracting data from various documents and retrieving data related to property and

equipment vouchers. By automating these tasks, the agency aims to increase efficiency and accuracy in data management.

3. **Customer Satisfaction and Efficiency Enhancement:** The vision of the IRS for RPA is to enhance customer satisfaction and improve operational efficiency. The agency intends to leverage RPA to streamline processes, reduce complexity, and provide enhanced decision-making support. Automation is a way to make the IRS more accessible, efficient, and effective for employees and taxpayers.

4. **Employee Upskilling and Reskilling:** As automation is integrated into IRS operations, the agency focuses on upskilling and reskilling its employees to work effectively with automation tools. This approach acknowledges that automation will change how tasks are performed, and the IRS aims to prepare its workforce for these shifts by enhancing their technical skills and soft skills, such as problem-solving and communication.

5. **Partnership with Chief Information Officer (CIO) Office:** To achieve successful automation

implementation, the text emphasizes the importance of collaboration between different divisions within the IRS. The finance and procurement departments work closely with the Office of the Chief Information Officer to select and implement the appropriate RPA software platform (UiPath in this case) and to guide staff in making informed decisions regarding automation capabilities.

6. **Change Management and Communication:** The IRS recognizes that successful automation requires effective change management and communication. The agency focuses on enhancing soft skills among its employees, encouraging open communication, and fostering collaboration. Clear communication and transparency are vital in managing the transition to an automated environment.

7. **Transition to Agile Finance:** The IRS views technology and automation as essential to its change to "agile finance," emphasizing innovation to meet future needs. Automation is a way to drive efficiency, enhance business decision support, and create a work environment where employees find value and career fulfillment.

This digital transformation initiative positively affects government operations and furthering scientific advances within the country. With free resources available through NASA's Open Data Initiative platform, anyone can now participate in invaluable knowledge exchange - opening up collaboration opportunities beyond traditional research institutes or universities.

U.S. Postal Service (USPS) Informed Delivery

For years, the United States Postal Service (USPS) has been a dependable source of mail services. But they recently completed one of America's most successful digital transformation projects ever set forth by the government - introducing Informed Delivery in April 2018.

This service notifies customers via email when their post arrives and even provides them with photos so they have a good idea of what to expect. On top of that, it gives people options for managing their mail before it reaches its destination – quite remarkable if you ask me.

Since its launch in 2018, the US Postal Service's service has been a fantastic success, with more than 19 million people signing up. It is still one of the most successful transformation projects due to its ease of use and user-friendly features. Not only does it provide a convenient way for customers to keep track of their mail deliveries, but they have also implemented various digital features such as tracking packages through text messages or emails and offering details about delivery online or using mobile applications. What other services could USPS offer that would make life easier?

USPS's Informed Delivery project has been a standout example of how government digital transformation can be successful. It effectively modernizes processes while maintaining customer satisfaction - two critical components for any successful program or initiative today.

With this, customers have been provided with an easier and more convenient way to receive essential packages and keep track of what's coming in and out of their mailbox daily without stepping outside or waiting at the post office all day. How amazing is it to stay up-to-date right from your own home?

Census Bureau's Digital Census

The Digital Census of the U.S. Census Bureau is one of the most successful digital transformation projects in the United States. It was launched back in 2020 to make sure that census data remains precise and up-to-date. This project utilizes advanced analytics, machine learning, cloud computing, and artificial intelligence to gather and analyze population statistics from all over America.

By monitoring changes over time with this information, we can accurately assess trends relating to population size or distribution within USA boundaries. So what does this mean? How will government entities apply these insights?

The Digital Census has been a massive hit since its launch. In the first year alone, it collected over 5 billion records. It includes all sorts of demographic information like gender, age group, race/ethnicity, and income level, which can then be used to devise public policies tailored to particular communities. And this data is not just helpful in helping create more effective government rules and supports economic development, such as job creation programs or housing projects targeting specific areas or populations. Couldn't we have done something like that earlier?

The Digital Census project not only collects demographic information from citizens across the U.S., but it also gives governments of all levels - from local townships to state ones - an improved understanding of their communities so that they can make better-informed decisions regarding public policy matters such as education spending and infrastructure investments. Moreover, this invaluable insight into how different features of a community are interconnected and have changed over time is something that would take expensive surveys or meticulous studies on individual topics otherwise. Finally, with A.I. & ML technologies in combination with traditional statistical methods for analysis – like when there are outliers – officials get access to comprehensive data, which helps them discern the requirements of their constituencies accurately and without heavy expenditure on manual processes like interviews or surveys.

The U.S. has demonstrated excellence in digital transformation projects and associated government-led initiatives. This strategy has enabled it to stay ahead of other nations by providing citizens with quick access to services online, boosting their convenience tremendously. As more countries enter into a digitized world, governments need to have no choice but embrace similar strategies if they want to remain successful on the global stage.

Chapter 3

Benefits of Intelligent Automation in Government

The world is undoubtedly changing, and naturally, so does the government sector. With technology advancing rapidly, intelligent Automation promises to revolutionize how governments operate. Several benefits associated with this form of Automation in public departments make it worth exploring - from streamlining processes to improving accuracy and efficiency and reducing costs for people at all levels. Intelligent Automation could also free up resources while cutting down on human error by allowing computers to take care of tasks that can be time-consuming or require a high precision rate when completed manually. By understanding these advantages of implementing such solutions to government operations, organizations will have insights into better decisions about using them correctly within their infrastructure.

Intelligent Automation in Government

Recently, the U.S. government has been relying heavily on sophisticated automation technologies like Robotic Process Automation (RPA), Artificial Intelligence (A.I.), and Machine Learning (ML). These new tools enable the gov to run more smoothly while cutting costs & eliminating staff.

For example, RPA can be used for document management systems & data entry in offices, plus streamline workflows with no human help involved. This tech is excellent when compiling legacy programs with newer ones, too - resulting in higher accuracy of information and increased flexibility overall.

Furthermore, Robotic process automation is utilized for fraud detection and compliance monitoring to automate further activities typically requiring massive manual effort. A.I. can be used to robotize decision-making processes by looking into vast amounts of organized or unstructured data to find trends or patterns that aid forecast results or solve potential problems. Moreover, A.I. makes it possible for more precise prognoses to consider multiple factors when estimating future outcomes, which humans cannot do due to their limited cognitive abilities.

The U.S. government is turning to machine learning for assistance in making better decisions more quickly than ever. This technology enables machines to identify patterns from a vast amount of data they work with daily - something that's beyond the abilities of humans because we can't handle such an immense volume and duration of info-processing. It's incredible what modern science can accomplish. What other ways are computers going to revolutionize our lives?

In addition, ML algorithms can learn from prior experiences and adjust if given new obstacles for them to overcome. It is known as "machine learning," which speeds up decision-making in an organization while not compromising accuracy or dependability. It's clear that intelligent automation technologies such as RPA, A.I. & ML are essential tools within government departments all over the U.S. now - they help save money while streamlining operations and ensuring accurate results simultaneously. Allowing governments worldwide access to this type of insight into their actions will enable them to make decisions faster than ever; it's a powerful resource.

Efficiency and Productivity Enhancement

Intelligent Automation is quickly becoming one of the most valuable tools for governments. Over the past few years, governments have seen an opportunity to use this technology to increase efficiency and productivity within their operations. Intelligent Automation offers a chance to streamline processes, reduce costs and enhance service delivery. Not only does intelligent Automation allow agencies better control of resources, but it also helps them reach their goals faster than before. At its essence, intelligent Automation comprises technologies that enable machines with more incredible speed and accuracy than humans are capable when taking on tasks alone - can you imagine how much quicker projects would be completed if we could combine human effort with machine intelligence?

These days, technology is advancing rapidly and delivering a whole host of new tools which can be used to automate mundane tasks. Robotic process automation (RPA), artificial intelligence (A.I.), (ML), and natural language processing (NLP) are just some examples of these cutting-edge technologies that allow organizations to get rid of manual effort from employees or other resources in completing tedious jobs quickly with accuracy.

Take the example of how government agencies have utilized intelligent Automation for expense management systems – it reflects this tech's impact on businesses so far. It's no wonder why more companies are taking advantage; streamlining processes lead to enhanced efficiency, cost savings, and improved customer experience - what's not to love? Not only does it free up your team members' time, enabling them to focus on value-added activities like exploring innovation opportunities, but it also boosts their morale by seeing how they work smarter instead of being held back by monotonous chores all day long.

Automating expense reporting processes with RPA solutions such as UiPath or Automation Anywhere allows governments to save time and improve accuracy. By using these automated systems, departments can process expenses faster while ensuring they're in line with policies across multiple locations - all without manually inputting each report into a centralized system. It eliminates tedious manual data entry tasks that take up valuable resources and prevents costly human errors associated with manual entries too.

Could we make this process even smoother?

Apart from making operations management more productive, intelligent Automation also offers fantastic options to enhance customer service within government agencies and give citizens direct access to the necessary information they require anytime through chatbots or other virtual assistants such as Amazon's Alexa or Google Home. This technology has made possible something that used to be unachievable earlier. To illustrate this point, with AI-driven chatbot solutions like IBM Watson Assistant and Microsoft Bot Framework in place, governments can now offer 24/7 customer support for their citizens without having actual humans on duty at all times - which goes a long way towards boosting citizen satisfaction while considerably cutting costs & time invested by departments of the administration.

Citizen-Centric Services

Intelligent Automation has been praised as the way of the future regarding government services. It promises greater efficiency and better outcomes for citizens. This technology is said to simplify providing services by streamlining processes, removing redundant or outdated steps, and cutting down on paperwork. Automating regular tasks such as filing forms or submitting documents can save money usually spent running a government agency while offering improved customer service - isn't that great?

Regarding citizen-centric services, the main goal is to provide citizens with access to resources and information that help them make decisions about their lives. Intelligent Automation from governments ensures this info is timely and personalized for each individual's needs. This way, people can get tailored advice based on what applies to their situation rather than generic advice for everyone. It gives citizens a better chance at finding solutions best suited for them instead of relying on a one-size-fits-all approach.

Right off the bat, intelligent Automation can offer a significant advantage by detecting potential issues before they become bigger problems requiring manual intervention from agency staff. Data security is of utmost importance when utilizing automated systems, so having proper safeguards such as encryption protocols and authentication measures are critical for protecting confidential data from any unauthorized access or misuse. It's also necessary to design user interfaces with an intuitive navigation system making it simple even for those not-so-familiar with technology to find what they're looking for without becoming overwhelmed by complicated menus or lengthy instructions.

Automated systems should fully utilize A.I. capabilities to improve accuracy and predict user needs based on behavior patterns.

Data-Driven Governance

Recently, Data-Driven Governance has been gaining much attention as governments worldwide recognize how powerful data and technology can be when making informed decisions. By collecting info from various sources, government officials can gain insight into what their citizens want and need to provide better services while maintaining transparency efficiently. Intelligent Automation is one tool used for successfully executing this manner of governance, which could result in more positive outcomes across the board. What's great about this approach is that it reduces cost and has other benefits like improved public service delivery.

Intelligent Automation utilizes artificial intelligence (A.I.) algorithms alongside analytics to automate tasks within government departments or agencies. It helps make workflows smoother by carrying out activities such as automatically creating reports or expediently responding to queries for information from citizens and other stakeholders. Utilizing A.I. also allows authorities to process a vast amount of data more promptly than possible, allowing them to make rationalized choices rapidly and efficiently. Have you ever wondered how much easier it could be if all these complex processes were automated? Imagine being able to find answers faster.

Moreover, incorporating intelligent Automation into government operations can help reduce human error while boosting accuracy in reporting and analysis, leading to better decision-making abilities. Automating tedious activities such as filing paperwork or retrieving documents saves time for more important stuff like creating policies or formulating strategies that would have taken too long if done by hand. Additionally, intelligent Automation lowers labor costs associated with specific processes, thereby increasing efficiency in an organization's budgetary framework while at the same time improving service delivery times overall. **How great is that?**

There are some great benefits to implementing Intelligent Automation, and Data-Driven Governance approaches in Government operations. It includes faster decision-making thanks to the increased speed of processing large amounts of data, reduced human error, significant cost savings on labor costs often associated with mundane tasks such as paperwork filing, etc., improved service delivery times across the board, and finally, freeing up time for more critical policy-making activities than manual ones. All these advantages demonstrate why Data-Driven Governance combined with Intelligent Automation could revolutionize how Governments operate today, bringing us closer to a future where governments can offer efficient services at every level due to intelligent automation technology being used throughout their procedures.

Ensuring Accuracy and Compliance

Maintaining accuracy and compliance is critical for government operations. However, with the increasing intricacy of laws, regulations, and data sources, it can be challenging to keep these standards up without an automated system in place. That's where Intelligent Automation comes into play. Utilizing A.I. and ML technologies, this type of Automation allows governments to rapidly process vast amounts of information while still adhering to high levels of accuracy and compliance - a significant benefit they wouldn't have access to otherwise. But how exactly does Intelligent Automation work?

By leveraging the power of artificial intelligence (A.I.) algorithms and machine learning (ML), these processes can function independently from human intervention or manual labor – ultimately reducing costs associated with manual effort while allowing more efficient use of resources.

Intelligent Automation enables governments to organize their regulatory systems better, allowing agencies to swiftly and accurately review regulations across different jurisdictions or regions. It means that all laws will be duly enforced regardless of where they are applied. Moreover, AI-powered technology ensures a faster-than-usual compliance process which is beneficial in terms of time efficiency and resource management for the government agency involved in the evaluation procedure. Would you agree that this could open up more accurate regulation enforcement opportunities?

Intelligent Automation revolutionizes how governments operate by allowing more efficient and accurate decision-making. It examines data more thoroughly than any human can do while offering predictive analysis models tailored explicitly to managing legal requirements such as tax codes or environmental regulations. This promising technology allows government departments to improve their services levels too, from promptly responding to customer queries via online portals or applications instead of having staff members take care them one at a time over days or weeks, depending on the staffing level available at a given moment, providing up-to-date information about offered service along with cost savings benefits since it eliminates manual labor expense - searching through documents to check compliance against existing laws & regulations – all these add up making intelligent Automation an essential component for modernizing organizations worldwide.

Cost Savings and Resource Allocation

Intelligent Automation in the government sector is taking off as a cost-saving measure and an effective resource allocation tool. This technology has allowed governments to become more efficient, reduce costs, and make sure resources are used where they can do the most good. Automation lets gov departments streamline their processes with fewer people needing to handle the same tasks. In addition, Automation allows for fast and accurate responses when needs change; this gives better customer service plus public services that match what citizens expect from them. Asking yourself how much time you'd save if your organization starts using Intelligent Automation.

Intelligent Automation comes in handy when it comes to saving money. Automated systems give you access to data from various sources, like internal databases, external resources such as social media sites, and other public databases. It allows for faster decision-making and more effective planning while allocating resources wisely. Moreover, automating specific processes eliminates manual labor associated with entering/collecting information which usually requires multiple personnel. As a result of these automated procedures, governments save time and money while still keeping accuracy levels high in their judgment calls - quite the smart move.

Intelligent Automation can be a big help to governments in terms of allocating resources. Instead of basing decisions solely on opportunity or budget constraints, this approach enables them to concentrate their efforts and funds more effectively where needed. This way increases efficiency while cutting down the spending that may not yield desired outcomes, such as investing too much money into projects which are optional or overstaffing specific departments with people who don't bring anything meaningful to the table. It's an exciting situation – how can we ensure our limited budgets go towards what will benefit us the most?

Intelligent Automation empowers governments to utilize their personnel efficiently, only when needed. It can help lower human error rates while ensuring that all employees are used optimally throughout the organization's activities based on evaluation algorithms considering current demand versus available capacity metrics and other factors. Furthermore, automated systems give organizations within the government sector, such as law enforcement agencies or intelligence bureaus, real-time information from various sources, allowing them to make instantaneous decisions without delay, resulting in faster response times when confronting urgent situations like terrorist threats, etc. Can these technologies deliver better safety? Will they eventually lead to improved decision-making processes during critical emergency scenarios?

Workforce Transition and Upskilling

The rise of intelligent Automation in government is transforming the workforce. People no longer think these positions will be safe and secure -- technology has changed how governments work drastically, so they're looking for ways to transition their current staff into roles more suitable for modern digital operations while developing new skill sets along the way. One significant advantage of using AI-driven solutions lies within its capacity: it can analyze vast volumes of data quickly and accurately. That brings a whole other level of efficiency which was not achievable before. Moreover, this newfound speed allows organizations to make decisions with confidence that would have taken significantly longer just a few years ago, getting ahead of trends much faster than ever before.

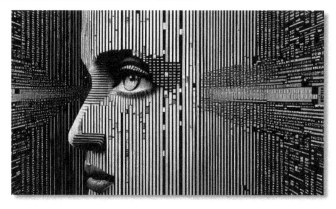

Thanks to Automation, governments have made their processes more efficient and make better decisions faster without relying on manual labor or complicated software solutions. Automation also provides them access to data from multiple sources simultaneously; this lets them take informed actions in real time, which would only be possible if done manually or via traditional software programs.

Moreover, intelligent Automation can help cut back expenses related to human resources by automating mundane tasks such as document processing or customer service roles, which often need an expensive workforce. Reducing the workload of personnel through automated procedures leaves extra time for employees who can concentrate on activities of higher value, like developing strategic plans or creating new services that will work much closer directly towards benefiting citizens.

Finally, intelligent Automation helps enhance operational efficiency, too, thanks to allowing quicker responses when dealing with queries by constituents, thus augmenting public trust within governing organizations while providing overall improved customer satisfaction plus forming a positive feedback loop between the government and its people.

Successful Case Studies in the U.S. Government

Intelligent Automation has completely changed how businesses from the public and private sectors function. Nevertheless, its implications are most visible in government organizations. Studies reveal that intelligent Automation amplifies accuracy while helping to achieve goals quicker within Government entities. Mainly, successful case studies from U.S. Administration clearly show how this technology helps make better decisions and increases transparency even as it simplifies processes with enhanced efficiency at a reduced cost.

An example of the power of intelligent Automation can be seen in the joint initiative between Intelligent Automation Incorporated (IAI) and the Department of Defense (DoD). By robotic process automation (RPA), DoD personnel could automate tedious manual tasks like data entry, document management, and customer service request processing with unprecedented speed and accuracy. It freed up resources for other higher-value functions within their organization, resulting in significant cost savings and improved response times for citizens relying on military services or benefits from Veterans Affairs programs.

The use of AI-assisted technologies such as natural language processing also bears fruit in U.S. Government operations, where it's employed by the Department of Homeland Security's Customs & Border Protection Agency (CBP). With machine learning algorithms that monitor large amounts of information taken from various sources simultaneously, they have been capable of effectively enhancing border security while making wait times shorter during airport inspections – an advantageous result both sides benefit significantly from.

Challenges and Mitigations

Intelligent Automation in government brings a great variety of advantages, but it also presents specific challenges that must be managed carefully. For instance, how do we ensure the personnel are educated and trained on using this technology? How can security for data and systems be provided when dealing with agencies with restricted I.T. budgets or who don't have enough personnel to manage such tasks? Fortunately, these organizations can use several strategies to overcome those issues.

To benefit fully from intelligent automation solutions, agencies must ensure their staff have adequate training and support. Vendors or other third-party providers often offer this program, so take advantage of that opportunity. Additionally, joining government-run forums is an excellent way for organizations to get feedback on the subject matter from colleagues who have already implemented such processes in their areas - thus allowing them to avoid reinventing the wheel.

Also, organizations should consider forming partnerships with private companies or other public entities when implementing intelligent automation solutions to their operations. Working together enables both parties to collaborate and use each other's resources and expertise for better results, reducing the risk and cost associated with implementation choices made solely by any party involved in this agreement. When it comes to security while executing an organization's automated solution, safety needs to be prioritized from the beginning stages – meaning sufficient authentication protocols must be established before transferring data into new systems or between departments within an agency's infrastructural framework. It is essential as without proper measures. Your sensitive information may fall prey easily, leading you to financial losses.

Conclusion

It's becoming increasingly clear that intelligent Automation is now an unavoidable part of government operations. Automation offers a range of advantages for governments, from streamlining processes and reducing costs to enhancing accuracy and compliance with regulations. Not only does this free up resources to be better utilized elsewhere, but it also means faster services provisioned more effectively - a win-win situation. Intelligent Automation could revolutionize how governments execute their tasks while simultaneously providing citizens with improved experiences; in the long run, what more motivation do you need?

Chapter 4

Challenges and Considerations for Intelligent Automation Adoption in Government

T
he demand for government organizations to provide citizens services more effectively and efficiently is growing, leading many of them to consider the adoption of intelligent automation. Implementing automated solutions in public departments can significantly improve efficiency, productivity and reduce costs. Nevertheless, this technology comes with its challenges and considerations that must be considered before adopting it.

Importance of intelligent automation in government operations

Intelligent automation uses technology to automate and optimize processes, allowing government organizations to become more efficient and effective in delivering services.

As governments endeavor to be increasingly agile in meeting resident needs, intelligent automation has become a fundamental instrument for transforming operations. Intelligent automation can lessen manual labor and streamline procedures, enabling government offices to concentrate on giving quality benefits at an economical expense.

Embracing intelligent automation presents both difficulties and opportunities for government associations alike. It offers tremendous potential but requires considering how it will fit into existing organizational systems and what practices should be implemented. Hence, its usage remains secure while achieving desired outcomes efficiently. Ultimately introducing any new tool or process comes down not only to keeping up with changing confinements yet additionally to perceiving where these innovative advances may support developing objectives requiring further exploration from leaders across all departments within an agency's structure.

When implementing an intelligent automation strategy, government organizations must monitor the potential benefits and risks associated with adoption. It means assessing their current IT capabilities; leveraging existing data sources; researching available tech solutions; gauging cost savings versus investments needed for the implementation process; taking necessary security measures such as encryption methods- all in line with applicable laws. It also means training staff on operating procedures and monitoring progress over time to ensure successful outcomes. Taking a holistic approach to developing an intelligent automation strategy can help governments make better decisions while minimizing risk exposure at the same time. On the one hand, we can reduce costs by eliminating manual labor or streamlining processes via algorithms or machine learning. Still, on the other, there is a need for investment into AI/ML technologies which may be outside the agency's budget right now, and shouldn't forget cybersecurity aspects either. Rhetorical questions like "How do you decide when technology brings more benefit than challenges?" naturally come up here, making us aware that investing thoughtfully upfront will pay off handsomely later.

Types of Intelligent Automation: RPA: AI: ML: Cognitive Automation

The government's adoption of intelligent automation technologies is increasing rapidly, becoming essential for digital transformation. IA consists of emerging techs used to automate labor-intensive and complex processes aiming to boost efficiency and reduce costs - these include RPA

(Robotic Process Automation), AI (Artificial Intelligence), Machine learning, and cognitive automation. Amongst them all, RPA shines with its use of software robots or "bots" that can handle repetitive tasks like customer service inquiries or data entry & document processing quickly and accurately.

AI and ML are two of the most critical technologies today. They can help improve accuracy, speed up processes, and even save costs when integrated into existing systems. AI is a way for computers to mimic human behavior, such as problem-solving or decision-making, without us having to input instructions manually every time – it's like teaching your computer how you would do something so they'll be able to learn by themselves over time. Meanwhile, Machine Learning uses algorithms that "learn" from training datasets, allowing them to complete specific tasks more efficiently than before - no need for manual programming changes each time.

These capabilities make AI and ML potent tools with an incredible range of applications across different industries, from healthcare services to financial investment analysis. The possibilities seem endless with these new technological advancements; who knows what could come next?

Cognitive automation is all about using technology like natural language processing and machine learning or vision to interpret text, images, or speech to make automated decisions on a large scale. It enables government organizations to implement Intelligence Artificial (IA) solutions without human intervention. However, several challenges need addressing when undertaking this process, notably security, access rights, and resources required for implementation - including personnel plus financial commitment.

These components must be managed appropriately from the outset due to potential delays or even project cancellations if not implemented correctly, so it pays dividends to consider carefully before embarking upon any IA endeavors.

Challenges in Intelligent Automation Adoption

Implementing intelligent automation technology by government bodies is a tricky task that needs several factors to be considered. Not only does it involve investing time and resources, but also considerable organizational adjustments as well. There could be many challenges while introducing the system in administration, such as keeping up with advancements in tech or finding funds for adoption projects – these are necessary elements for decision-makers to learn before taking on this venture. It means there's a lot that they need to consider when embarking upon implementing an AI-powered solution within their operations.

A significant obstacle that must be conquered before intelligent automation can enter government agencies is the need for more staff awareness and training associated with modern technology. It's crucial for workers to possess essential technical skills in artificial intelligence, machine learning, robotics process optimization (RPA), or other forms of automated reasoning; however, they should also have a thorough grasp of these technologies if they are going to use them correctly within their organization's environment. So how do we get employees up-to-speed?

How will it benefit our organizations when AI solutions become mainstream?

Several factors must be considered when implementing intelligent automation into a government organization. One of the most important things is providing enough training and resources for staff members to develop their skills before anyone starts using new systems or solutions. After all, we don't want any accidental errors in our operations. Another factor that needs consideration is security concerns. With governments relying increasingly on digital data systems for their operations, the risks associated with storing sensitive information online and using automated processes within that system become even higher. Is there anything else we should look out for?

Organizations must ensure they have the proper measures to protect their data from cyber-attacks and breaches. These include authentication protocols, encryption methods, and access controls - all while meeting desired performance levels with automated solutions. Cost is another factor that needs to be considered when introducing intelligent automation; it includes the initial purchase of tools or services and ongoing operational costs like maintenance fees and subscription charges (in the case of cloud-hosted services). If these expenses are not appropriately managed during an automated system's lifespan, they can become expensive very quickly, making budgeting accurately before implementation critical for long-term success.

Considerations for Successful Adoption

Considering the adoption of intelligent automation in government can be a tricky process. It takes careful thought and planning to ensure everything goes when introducing this tech to departments. There are tons of things that need to factor into consideration, with cost being one of the main ones. Sure, you may save on operational costs, but it's essential to decide if those savings will outweigh what it'll take for implementation throughout every department. Doing so is critical before taking further steps forward.

What's more, organizations should also bear in mind the potential additional costs necessary for training employees and keeping the system updated after it is implemented. Government agencies must be cautious regarding security and compliance requirements since they are governed by strict regulations regulating data privacy and security and must follow national laws or policies. That being said, before implementing an automated system, these law considerations need to be taken into account with the help of legal professionals from each agency. Lastly, when introducing intelligent automation, organizations must evaluate if existing resources will deliver successful adoption across all departments involved or if further hardware/software investments will be required.

Future Trends and Directions

Intelligent automation is quickly becoming a valid option for government organizations to become more effective and agile in their workflow. It can help manage operations, save money and improve services provided to citizens. But it's important to remember that with the adoption of intelligent automation come specific challenges that must be tackled before beginning implementation. Future trends or developments must be the most significant factor when introducing this technology into government organizations. As tech continues advancing faster than ever, governments must stay ahead by predicting changes within their sector as soon as possible; being prepared could mean adapting rapidly and cutting costs while still delivering high-quality results.

Staying in the loop of all new emerging technologies like (AI), (ML), Natural Language Processing (NLP), Robotic Process Automation (RPA), and Blockchain Solutions is essential for organizations. This way, they can decide which would suit their needs, as these are becoming more commonplace across various industries. But at the same time, it's also essential that governments keep security measures in mind while utilizing any such technology so that users still have a smooth experience with high-end safety protocols intact. Cybersecurity must always be top of mind when introducing new systems or tools into existing procedures — even minor mistakes can severely affect public trust and compliance with data security regulations. On top of that, governments should think about the scalability of any solution they take on – making sure it is flexible enough to handle future needs without significant changes or updates later down the line; this will also guarantee long-term savings compared to having to buy an entirely different system every few years due to lack of scalable options offered by-products in the market today. Have we done enough research before picking a product? Are its features sufficient for our current requirements and foreseeable growth patterns?

Conclusion

Adopting intelligent automation in government is a complex task. It requires careful consideration of all available challenges and opportunities before any decision can be made on an automated strategy. Governments must also understand this technology well to ensure its potential implications are considered when developing a plan tailored specifically for their operations. Furthermore, they must analyze which specific tasks could best benefit from automation, how resources should optimally be allocated, and what measures need to be put in place regarding data security concerns - doing so will help them increase efficiencies while reducing costs simultaneously. With thoughtful planning beforehand, intelligent automation has real potential for making things more accessible now and in the future – but proper studies must occur first.

Chapter 5

Leveraging Generative AI in Public Services

Generative AI has rapidly become a trending topic since more and more companies are incorporating this technology into their public services. The perks of generative AI can be immense, from service automation to enhanced performance and cost-saving advantages. We will investigate some of the manners in which generative AI can be applied within public services, revealing all the different opportunities and difficulties connected with these technologies. We'll also study how firms can optimize their potential gains by utilizing generative AI. Is your business exploring ways you could use Generate Artificial Intelligence? What challenges might come with it?

Importance of Generative AI in transforming public services

Generative AI is a technology that carries the potential to revolutionize public services. It promises greater efficiency, cost savings, and improved customer satisfaction by automating processes previously requiring manual labor. It could mean governments can spend more time on what's important: providing citizens with reliable and efficient services while cutting costs in the long run - an attractive prospect. But how exactly will generative AI shape our existing public service infrastructure?

One way it can be used is for predictive analytics, predicting future trends based on current data sets so proactive solutions can be developed before problems arise. Generative AIs can also recognize patterns from large databases, allowing officials to understand their users' needs better and identify areas needing improvement within specific departments or programs. In addition, they will free up staff to focus on creative tasks instead of mundane ones like simple paperwork filing – something many workers dread doing anyway. So why not put this power into practice sooner rather than later?

Speed is the primary advantage of employing artificial intelligence (AI). It's much quicker than people when it comes to performing specific duties like data processing or decision-making. It makes AI perfect for quickly and precisely dealing with enormous amounts of information without more human resources. Not only that, but results produced by machines are less biased than if they were made manually - decisions are based on facts rather than feelings which decreases the chance for unfairness in services provided by governing bodies to its citizens. Rhetorical question: Does everyone want unbiased processes?

Generative AI is revolutionizing decision-making processes for government officials, allowing them to access more data faster and smoother than traditional methods like surveys or interviews. Its improved accuracy also means they can make better decisions because unbiased information allows the people of power to understand their constituents' thoughts on specific issues and policies without needing to analyze each case personally. Using generative AI in public services helps modernize governments to offer citizens solutions that fit their needs optimally while staying ahead of competitors who may still need to adopt similar technologies. It keeps everyone up-to-date about current technology trends.

Applications in Public Services:

Generative AI is a powerful tool becoming increasingly essential for public services. It can be used to generate, customize and enhance data in new ways, which helps streamline the delivery of public services more effectively and precisely. Generative AI has lots of potential for adding creativity into providing public service; think artwork, virtual assistants, or chatbots. Generatively-based Artificial Intelligence (AI) particularly excels in content generation and personalization - both processes involve using NLP techniques to create original material from existing sources and structured databases.

Generative AI benefits public services, especially those that need dynamic content like news or blogs. Personalization using NLP technology also plays a vital role in helping public services provide tailored experiences based on the user's wants and needs. Data augmentation and synthesis are other key areas where this type of AI can also be used. It takes all the data available about users, so it can give them personalized recommendations, which makes their experience much better since they don't have to search through tons of info themselves. Isn't that amazing? Generative AI brings lots of convenience regarding understanding people's preferences to get precisely what you want from your service provider without hassle - quite efficient, right? Data augmentation involves applying NLP algorithms to existing data sets to create new info from available sources. This process helps organizations gain value quickly without having access to or requiring manual creation processes for large datasets. Data synthesis takes it one step further by using machine learning and AI models to generate novel datasets from the ground up.

Leveraging this capability enables government agencies or healthcare providers to develop realistic yet fictionalized databases that can be used for training ML models while protecting real-world privacy concerns connected with sensitive data found within actual databases. How cool is that?

Generative AI is changing how we do things, and it's become evident in newer technologies such as virtual assistants and chatbots. Virtual assistants provide quick access to specific information while also being able to tailor their guidance based on user input. Chatbots, meanwhile, allow automated conversations that are communicated through text messages via websites or social networks - making them incredibly useful for customer service departments. They help reduce costs associated with hiring additional staff; they can handle numerous queries simultaneously due to their automation capabilities – talk about efficiency.

Benefits and Impact

Generative AI is on the rise as it has incredible potential to deliver new and creative solutions for public services. It combines data-driven insights, machine learning algorithms, and Natural Language Processing (NLP) technologies to get original ideas or content. These days, generative AI can be used in various ways, from crafting marketing campaigns tailored to customer demands and giving personalized recommendations based on their interests to generating predictive models that anticipate what customers need even before they do. How neat would it be to know what our consumers wanted?

Government agencies can benefit from higher efficiency and cost savings by using generative AI in public services while ensuring better citizen outcomes. Generative AI may aid in discovering data patterns that could lead to enhanced decision-making within an organization or even propose brand-new ways of dealing with complex issues such as poverty or homelessness. For instance, it might be employed to locate regions where people require the most help and then put forward relevant interventions accordingly. What's more, by using this technology, organizations can deliver improved results without wasting time on redundant operations - all while catering precisely tailored solutions for their citizens' needs.

Generative AI has great potential, like creating personalized messages that get sent out automatically when certain conditions are met. It could send emergency alerts during natural disasters or notify people who may qualify for assistance programs - two essential services. It can also make life easier by providing more tailored and relevant information based on each individual's needs. By utilizing (NLP) technology and machine learning algorithms, public service providers can give better advice specific to an individual's circumstances rather than just showing everyone the same generic message from their organization.

This technology offers citizens more control, with access to accurate information quickly and without having to manually fill out forms or wait in line at a government office. It benefits everyone by increasing decision-making accuracy while improving user experience explicitly tailored toward individual needs. It is why it has been embraced by different countries looking into increasing efficiency across the board, all while ensuring better outcomes for their citizens - which explains its rising popularity.

Implementing Generative AI in Public Services

In recent years, the use of generative AI in public services has gained much attention and has been heavily focused on by research & development teams. It can be used to create new opportunities for public service providers by taking a data-driven approach to problem-solving. Generative AI looks at datasets from those providers and spots patterns that allow them to develop fresh solutions or products - opening up possibilities they may not have seen before. Could this pave the way for more responsive and effective government organizations?

Using generative AI, public service providers have the potential to cut down expenses related to creating new services or products from scratch. Moreover, it can improve the reliability of existing products and help decision-makers make better decisions in less time by providing them with a way to go through vast amounts of data quickly and accurately. Think about this if you work for the public sector: instead of spending hours reviewing hard-to-gauge information -what if you could get actionable insights immediately? It would allow a more efficient decision-making process within any public organization.

What can generative AI do? Well, it's capable of predicting future trends and helping organizations plan. It looks into current trends more effectively than traditional methods alone, allowing them to get a better picture of what the next steps should be. Furthermore, this technology is increasingly used in public services such as payroll systems, customer relations management (CRM), and workflow automation systems – providing an efficient way to streamline those administrative processes.

Generative algorithms can be trained on existing datasets, allowing them to identify patterns to guide their decisions when dealing with administrative tasks. It could include routing customers or automatically assigning tasks based on user preferences and history for increased efficiency throughout the organization workflow process. In short, there is a ton of potential when it comes to leveraging generative AI in public services, from reducing costs associated with creating new products/services from scratch, improving decision-making processes through automated analysis, and predicting future trends more accurately than traditional methods alone, - all leading to enhanced optimization of administrative functions. Organizations that take advantage of this technology have an edge over their competition – positioning themselves well toward success now and into the future.

Future Prospects and Implications

Generative AI is shaking up how public services are provided. Automated systems are revolutionizing how governments and other organizations carry out their operations by creating new solutions and capabilities that meet specific needs, reduce costs, and make things more efficient. Generative AI can be utilized to streamline complex procedures such as data analysis, natural language processing (NLP), computer vision (CV), speech recognition (SR) & robotics - offering service providers an unprecedented understanding of what works best for their constituents. What does this mean in terms of cost savings? Increased efficiency in addressing public demands? It's an exciting opportunity.

Generative AI has the potential to vastly cut down costs that come with public services by automating complex tasks which otherwise need lots of human labor or resources. Take natural language processing, for instance; generative AI can allow government agencies to reply much faster and more accurately than ever before in response to people's inquiries without creating a team whose sole purpose is this. Furthermore, CV technology could enable automated facial recognition systems at places like airports or government buildings without needing the constant presence of pricey personnel. Can you imagine how quickly international travel would become if security lines weren't so backed up?

Finally, robotics powered by generative AI have the potential to automate tasks that are usually carried out manually, such as landscaping or custodial work. This way, government agencies can free up financial resources while still providing quality service in these areas. Moreover, governments may benefit from increased transparency through analytics platforms driven by generative AI and track how citizens interact with different initiatives over time. This data gives an insight into where improvements can be made, and it allows agencies to understand better what their constituents need if they choose to implement new policies or projects for them down the line. Not only does this help ensure programs achieve desired outcomes, but it also provides valued feedback that helps shape future decisions.

Conclusion

AI is becoming a more significant part of our lives, and leveraging generative AI can help us automate processes and make them more efficient. Generative AI is a precious tool that helps improve public services in various ways. For example, it reduces costs for all involved parties, saves time when accessing the resources you need, and makes these services much easier to use overall. With proper implementation techniques, this technology could open up plenty of new opportunities for citizens and businesses.

Chapter 6

Use Cases of IA and Gen AI in Government Operations

The implementation of Intelligent Automation (IA) and General Artificial Intelligence (Gen AI) in government operations is becoming more noticeable. These technologies can automate routine tasks, create extra resources, and make better decision-making, which explains why governments are resorting to them for help. It looks into several IA and Gen AI use cases in governmental processes like automated documentation management or predictive analytics.

Importance of Intelligent Automation (IA) and General Artificial Intelligence (Gen AI)

Realizing the importance of Intelligent Automation (IA) and General Artificial Intelligence (Gen AI), their usage in government operations is increasing daily. This growing popularity is due to these technologies' capability to smoothen processes, optimize operational efficiency, and reduce financial costs. IA merges robotics with computer visioning, natural language processing, and machine learning to help automate tasks that need regular attention but are small enough not to require a human's direct intervention. At the same time, Gen AI can think independently & make decisions without any manual control from humans involved. For governmental functions specifically, IA can be used proficiently for automating repetitive chores such as data entry or document management that might consume a humongous amount of time otherwise; however, they're vital factors for different departments functioning effectively within an organization.

Integrating AI and General Artificial Intelligence into government operations significantly has enormous potential when streamlining processes that don't require an individual's attention. It could be an excellent way for governments to save resources, which can be put towards more complex activities. Also, with predictive analytics being made possible by these technologies – trends in large datasets or correlations between different factors are much easier identified than done manually by people, thus giving us quicker results.

Even better is how this technology has been shown to reduce bias due to their independent decision-making capabilities based solely on data rather than emotion or opinion–which we all know humans tend to let influence decisions either consciously or unconsciously. So, IA makes government operations faster and more accurate than doing things without it, helping taxpayers save money in labor costs and minimizing costly mistakes if caught earlier before implementation.

Use Cases of Intelligent Automation (IA) in Government Operations:

IA has a lot of applications in government operations. One of the most popular ones are administrating tasks, providing citizen services, and enforcing compliance with regulations. Automation can help simplify complex administrative processes - it provides tools for automated workflows, collecting data, tracking task completions, document management, and reporting. It makes such processes faster while cutting down on manual labor costs simultaneously. IA also finds its use when delivering citizens' services – why not take advantage of modern technology?

AI-powered chatbots can make life much easier for citizens by providing instant information about government services or programs. No more long wait times on hold, no need to visit the office - it's all at your fingertips, which is super convenient. It also helps reduce the burden of responding directly to each inquiry separately from government personnel.

Regarding compliance and regulations, AI can help governments stay within legal boundaries while efficiently operating. Solutions such as predictive analytics allow governments an insight into potential issues before they become actual problems so that appropriate action can be taken when required preventing any risk associated with noncompliance violations or other regulatory breaches – isn't that amazing?

Use Cases of General Artificial Intelligence (Gen AI) in Government Operations:

Have you ever heard of General Artificial Intelligence (Gen AI)? This technology has taken the world by storm - with governments across the globe using it to improve their operations and serve citizens better. Gen AI is used in various areas, from policy analysis and decision-making to innovative city management, public safety, and security. It's even capable of 'seeing' patterns within vast amounts of data that would otherwise be invisible through traditional methods. Talk about having a supercomputer brain.

Predictive analytics helps governments make better decisions when making policies affecting large populations. For example, the government has used predictive analytics along with Gen AI to find out where its existing public policies need changing or fine-tuning to meet its citizens' needs better. This same technology is also being implemented in innovative city management projects like traffic control systems and energy efficiency plans to benefit those living within a particular area. What kinds of changes would people be able to see if more cities adopted these types of initiatives? How might it improve our day-to-day lives?

Cities can create systems that accurately predict future scenarios based on past data patterns. It could help them optimize resources while minimizing costs associated with waste or over-consumption of energy sources. Gen AI can also improve public safety and security by helping law enforcement authorities via facial recognition technology or other automated surveillance systems, which can detect suspicious behavior much faster than humans alone ever could. Moreover, predictive policing algorithms created using Gen AI allow police forces around the globe to monitor crime hotspots so they're better equipped when necessary. They may even prevent potential crimes from occurring in the first place through preventive measures like increased patrolling activities within certain areas where criminal activity has a higher chance of taking place.

Benefits of Integrating IA and Gen AI in Government Operations

The integration of Intelligent Automation (IA) and General Artificial Intelligence (Gen AI) into government operations has been rushed in recent years. It is down to growing access to data, improvements in machine learning algorithms, and governments' need to act more efficiently and effectively. By combining these two powerful technologies, governments can enjoy several benefits that would be difficult or impossible through conventional methods alone. One example could be more efficient handling and analysis of data.

Using IA and Gen AI in government processes can help save time, money, and effort. Automating the analysis of large datasets or automatically generating reports based on the data are great examples of how this technology can streamline tasks that would take humans much longer to complete. Furthermore, sophisticated algorithms may be able to uncover hidden patterns or make predictions that could otherwise go unnoticed without automated assistance helping governments target areas for improvement more effectively than ever before. Adding such technologies into decision-making is also incredibly beneficial as it helps ensure accuracy – an invaluable asset when dealing with complex governance challenges.

Governments can generate more precise models for predicting outcomes using machine learning algorithms such as deep neural networks rather than manual methods alone. It can result in greater accuracy when assessing projects, programs, services, etc., and better distribution of resources among departments and agencies within a government organization. What implications does this have? Increased precision means that decisions made by the government become based on reliable predictions rather than subjective opinion or gut feeling - something which could potentially be very beneficial for citizens worldwide. Not only will people receive fairer treatment from their state, but they will also see improvements concerning the provision of essential services like healthcare and education.

IA and Gen AI can help save some money by automating tasks that people used to do - like document processing or customer service inquiries.

Then they could use their personnel resources elsewhere while still getting the desired results with minimal human involvement once everything is set up. Plus, if they put big data analytics together with predictive modeling techniques, then organizations have a chance to anticipate future trends, which will help them stay in front of the competition plus lower the costs of responding too late when something changes around them.

Challenges and Considerations

Implementing IA and Gen AI in government operations has brought many challenges and considerations. To successfully utilize technology, stakeholders must discuss data collection, purpose, access, and legal implications before proceeding with projects. With so many factors at play here, questions arise: Are we ready for such drastic changes? What safeguards do we need to put in place? Only time will tell, but one thing's sure – any decision made needs consideration from every angle possible.

Regarding storing or transmitting sensitive information, privacy concerns must be considered due to the potential cyber security risks. It is especially true for governments, which must protect citizens from any misuse or abuse of data collected through AI and Gen AI applications. It's important to regularly audit data collection and use encryption techniques to reduce risk. Accountability measures must be put in place for those overseeing these technologies. Also, governments have an ethical obligation too. They need to consider the implications of incorporating artificially intelligent systems into their decision-making process and develop safeguards against potential bias or discrimination that could arise from applying this technology. Moreover, they should consider not only ethics but also what kind of impact AI might have on society overall; both desirable and undesirable outcomes must be considered while making decisions about its utilization within governmental affairs.

Future Trends and Potential

Recently AI and general AI have been gaining more recognition for their use in the government sector. New technologies are being developed to help governments realize the potential advantages of these tools, such as automation which helps improve operational efficiency. But governments must be equipped with a good understanding of current trends and possible applications when considering implementation; this will ensure they're prepared for any issues they may face. So what does this mean? How can governments make sure they're ready to adopt these new technologies? We must keep educated on how artificial intelligence advances so that public-sector organizations and citizens benefit from its proper application in our daily lives.

NLP, or natural language processing, is already having a significant effect on the operations of governments. It helps computers understand our languages, which can then be used for document analysis, voice recognition, and other tasks by government departments to automate them to save time while keeping precision intact. Besides this, NLP also finds its use in text analytics which aids decision-makers in getting an insight into public opinion regarding various policies or programs. How valuable must it be for leaders worldwide with access to such technology?

Virtual agents are becoming increasingly popular within government organizations as people find it convenient to interact directly with machines without needing a live person. This helpful technology can be used to fulfill basic tasks such as providing information about services or quick answers if someone has any queries regarding their experience with governmental organizations' service offerings.

Machine learning (ML) will evolve more common in our lives over time - what implications this could have remains unknown. ML makes it possible for computers to learn from data sets without needing specific programming instructions. It allows them to base their predictions on past experiences or patterns discovered in large datasets, which can be helpful in areas such as healthcare policymaking and national security decisions where there is a need for data-driven insights, but obtaining the necessary information with surveys may not always be feasible because of privacy issues or cost constraints. Can AI help us make better-informed choices? Or will it lead to unintended consequences?

GANs have a role to play in government operations. These networks train algorithms on large datasets of images and random noise inputs provided by computer scientists. It would enable machines to generate life-like pictures from the bottom up - no need for real photos. Government agencies could then benefit from facial recognition tech without having to take photographs themselves; instead, they'd get descriptions provided directly by citizens making sure that privacy concerns remain at bay while still being accurate enough for security checks, etcetera, at airports or other practical needs. That sounds like an exciting way of keeping both accuracy and privacy balanced.

Conclusion

AI and Gen AI have the potential to revolutionize government operations. Automating mundane tasks can free up resources for more critical activities, while wise decision-making could lead to better public services. However, governments must ensure they put effective governance in place before leveraging these technologies to protect citizens' data privacy and guarantee ethical usage at all times. With a suitable approach, implementing AI and GenAI will create improved services and ensure cost savings – an opportunity too good for any government to pass out on.

Chapter 7

AI Applications in Government Decision Making

I t is an era of fast technology. Artificial Intelligence (AI) is getting involvement in government decisions. AI systems utilize to take over complex tasks. It provides better solutions and insight for making decisions. All over the world, governments have started exploring the concept 'Of AI Governance. It makes their work easy and efficient.

Introduction to AI in Government Decision Making

AI is emerging as a critical component in government decision-making. Governments recognize AI's potential to dramatically boost efficiency, lower costs, and make better choices that benefit citizens. With AI, governments can now analyze massive amounts of data more quickly than they ever could manually - making for reliable conclusions drawn from those findings. What's more? It can also add greater transparency and accountability to decisions by accurately recording why certain decisions were taken, yielding positive results.

AI has become a powerful tool when it comes to data. It can quickly identify patterns, trends, and correlations that may have been overlooked or not easily accessible by humans - giving organizations the ability to respond rapidly in times of crisis or urgent matters. This technology is being adopted across multiple sectors; governments use AI for budget management, improved public services, security threat detection, fraud prevention, and more. This technology's incredible potential is incredible – we've only scratched the surface so far.

For instance, in India's Kerala state government's budgeting process, AI was used to evaluate how money had been spent and utilized over recent years to ascertain its effect on citizens' lives. Similarly, Australia's Northern Territory government employs AI to identify fraudulent activity or misuse of healthcare funds/resources. Besides the applications that governments already have adopted worldwide, there are still many possible uses waiting to be discovered with further research like automated legal assistants, which could help lawyers from within the system; predictive analytics, which departments such as transportation or education can adopt; natural language processing tools aiding document drafting processes and machine learning algorithms being instrumental in spotting any gaps present inside existing policies etcetera. That being said, what else would you say lie ahead?

Data collection and preprocessing:

Gathering and organizing data for ML models used in policy analysis is critical. Data from various sources must be brought together, filtered out of errors or undesired elements, and structured into an accessible form. This process could involve normalizing the data set, eliminating extreme values that don't fit the pattern, and designing new features out of existing ones. Additionally, NLP approaches are helpful when tackling sentiment analyses connected with policies based on text material.

Natural Language Processing (NLP) techniques give us the power to get valuable information from text documents by analyzing words and phrases for what they mean in their context, how they make people feel when reading, or even whether a positive or negative sentiment is attached. For example - we want to understand public opinion on a particular policy issue; NLP algorithms could help identify related topics within that document and analyze if any statements made have either a positive or negative undertone. Policymakers can then use these insights before making important decisions regarding this particular matter. In other words - What do people think? How does it affect them? Is there potential support for specific ideas? All these questions become answerable thanks to the data gathered from Natural Language Processing tools.

AI applications have become a critical component of government decision-making these days. Their ability to automate complex tasks with far greater accuracy than human capabilities make them invaluable, not least because AI models are immune to the biases and errors that come from fatigue or stress, which can plague humans when it comes to decision-making. Additionally, they open up access for governments to real-time insights into large datasets - something impossible due to its sheer scale beyond what an individual could process accurately and efficiently enough for timely decisions in areas like budget allocation based on macroeconomic indicators over expansive timescales such as months or even years. In short, without the computational power provided by AI technology today, achieving both tactical objectives in the short term while simultaneously working towards long-term economic goals, such as growth maximization while upholding social welfare standards, would be next to impossible.

AI-Powered Predictive Analytics for Public Safety

As governments struggle to navigate the ever-rising complexity of decisions they're confronted with, Artificial Intelligence (AI) is becoming an increasingly attractive option for public sector decision-making. Predictive analytics powered by AI can offer officials a window into current and future potential situations that otherwise would be unexplored. An example of how AI could be applied in the government's decision-making process is predictive policing models, which help us comprehend crime trends more effectively and take preemptive action if needed. How might this technology evolve further? It indeed has exciting potential.

Predictive policing models utilize machine learning algorithms and massive amounts of data to detect criminal behavior across geographic regions or populations over a period. This helps police officers take preemptive steps against possible future felonies before they even occur. Additionally, these models enable allocating resources better by determining areas with higher rates of crime that might need more law enforcement presence or different interventions aimed at reducing the crime rate.

The data utilized for predictive policing models typically incorporate past crime reports, demographic information, social media posts, economic indicators, weather states of affairs, traffic data, and other public records associated with criminal activity. By examining these datums in concert with each other using AI calculations such as managed learning (e.g., KNN), unmanaged learning (e.g., clustering), or even deep-learning techniques (e.g., convolutional neural networks), it is likely to construct precise predictions about where wrongdoings are apt to happen and how best police officers should answer so they can keep them from occurring initially. To be able to make effective preventive decisions utilizing artificial intelligence methods, one must have access to reliable datasets containing vital information related to the nature of crimes that could occur soon - this includes not only previous incidents but also various factors like climate conditions, which may lead increase risk rate periods marked by high criminality level.

AI-Driven Resource Allocation and Planning;

AI technology has enabled government decision-makers to create more efficient resource allocation and planning solutions. The AI-driven applications have entirely transformed how governments make decisions, allowing them to plan for future requirements while allocating resources based on real-time needs. Moreover, Artificial Intelligence is an effective tool for automating optimally allotting resources, which was earlier handled by specialists who made manual calculations.

AI systems can successfully predict how much demand there will likely be for specific kinds of resources, thus helping identify areas where extra capacity is necessary. Furthermore, such technologies even assist infrastructure planners by utilizing past data-related information to simulate different scenarios and decide optimal outcomes.

AI can be used to make sense of intricate data from various sources, which would help create better models for optimizing the allocation of resources. This type of analysis makes life easy for governments as they can understand the likely effects before investing significantly in any project or policy initiative, thus leading to more informed decisions. In this way, AI proves its ability to improve decision-making processes and yield positive results. Have you ever experienced how incorporating AI into your operations has improved things?

Using AI in government decision-making also enables greater visibility regarding resource management and better responsibility from chosen representatives when it comes time to allocate finances or resources towards important schemes or initiatives that offer advantages for constituents overall. Governments are increasingly accepting AI-driven resolutions since they have come to know its possible profits, such as savings on expenses, added productivity, and advanced precision in forecasting models and reenactments that direct policy decisions at all administration stages. How can governments harness the potential benefits of these cutting-edge technology solutions? Can this help us reach a more efficient way forward by investing scarce resources into mission-critical projects?

Governments can quickly access insights from large datasets with the rise of automated audits using robotic process automation (RPA) and artificial intelligence tools such as natural language processing systems. It is a vast improvement on traditional methods that could have been more time-consuming and efficient. As more organizations incorporate AI into their decision-making processes, they will be better equipped to predict trends - both in the short term and long term – which can benefit citizens now while also setting them up for success years down the line, ultimately resulting in improved outcomes for everyone involved, including taxpayers who rely on government officials to make sound investments with public money allocated towards projects that would carry society forward into future times.

Ethical and Governance Considerations

As governments and the public sector continue to move towards utilizing Artificial Intelligence (AI) for decision-making, specific ethical and governance considerations must be taken into account. Fairness, transparency, and accountability should be prioritized when making decisions with AI in government contexts. Additionally, we cannot overlook the potential impacts of using AI on human rights protection, privacy issues, or data security; these elements must also be addressed. How can a machine's output ensure adherence to every single right granted by law? Can an algorithm provide the same impartiality for people subjected to scrutiny, no matter their background? These questions must also bear consideration when dealing with such complex topics.

Creating a framework that outlines particular rules and processes for using this tech is necessary to ensure that ethical standards are observed when using AI in government decision-making. This framework should comprise instructions on how data should be obtained, saved, and used; how algorithms must be crafted; what steps need to be taken to combat bias; how outcomes created by AI systems ought to be openly conveyed - who will bear responsibility for them and also ways feedback loops can help such systems better over time.

Moreover, governments have got some other matters they have a look at related to economic effects brought up by automation technologies like job losses or labor market changes due to either displacement or improved productivity, plus social limitations such as widening digital gaps between those having access technology vs those without any accessibility. Not only that, but public sector organizations require robust oversight mechanisms so administrative officials may effectively monitor applications involving AI while still allowing enough liberty for advancement within existing laws yet being certain conformity is attained concerning international norms linked disciplines, including protection of human rights & privacy regulations associated with data handling.

Conclusion

AI Governance, Government AI, Decision Making AI, and Automated Decisions are all facets of the burgeoning trend to use Artificial Intelligence in government decision-making. By exploiting the data-driven intelligence that advanced algorithms provide, governments can make their operations more efficient and effective. Improved accuracy, expedited rate, and cost efficiency-- are a few advantages for authorities that adopt such modern technologies. Indeed, using Artificial Intelligence based decisions will have an essential role in the future when operating administrations at different levels. What's also worth noticing here is how this technology helps reveal potential problems while pinpointing cause-and-effect correlations – something that humans may either miss out on or overlook altogether.

Chapter 8

Security and Risk Management in IA Implementation

In the contemporary tech-savvy era, various risks and threats must be managed. As global connectivity grows exponentially, companies should take a proactive approach toward security and risk management for successful Information Architecture (IA) implementation. With numerous malicious actors posing cyber hazards daily, organizations should comprehend how to reduce potential safety issues while implementing IA.

Understanding Security and Risks in IA Implementation:

As organizations move towards a more automated approach to process management, they must ponder the security risks of instituting Intelligent Automation (IA). IA is an effective instrument that allows companies to mechanize different activities and systematize processes; however, it creates potential security imperatives. To ensure that one's organization is suitably defended against these dangers, it is essential for one to comprehend the assorted kinds of safety concerns related to IA establishment and how best to reduce their effects.

Data protection must be of utmost priority. Solid encryption algorithms and authentication protocols must be utilized when implementing IA solutions to safeguard against any vulnerability from storing data within the system. Furthermore, organizations should consider deploying physical access controls to deter malicious attacks or thwart unauthorized attempts at accessing them from external entities. In addition, due consideration must be given to protecting organizational systems from insider threats just as much as those stemming externally, such as hacking efforts or malware infection.

Organizations must protect their information assets, such as instituting adequate access controls for users and monitoring user activity on the system for any indications of malicious behavior. Additionally, frequent vulnerability assessments should be conducted to identify weaknesses or possible points of failure which could lead to a breach of confidential data or other valuable resources within an organization's network environment. Organizations must also consider legal ramifications related to IA implementation by ensuring they adhere to existing laws and regulations covering privacy protection and safeguarding information. For instance, some countries may necessitate extra safeguards beyond those generally employed for everyday operations inside an organizational system network due to particular rules regarding data storage or transfer across borders.

Mitigating Security Risks in IA Implementation:

The security and risk management of an intelligent automation (IA) implementation is critical to consider when constructing a successful IA program. Security risks must be addressed in the first instance, as they can have considerable implications for the success of the IA deployment. Primarily, the focus must be placed on authentication and authorization processes which will help guarantee that only sanctioned users may gain access to confidential data or systems. Moreover, measures such as data encryption and protection ought to exist to prevent any unauthorized access or interference with sensitive information.

Finally, regular security audits and penetration testing should be performed to identify potential vulnerabilities that could compromise the integrity of an IA implementation. These tests can determine whether authentication processes are up-to-date in terms of requiring multiple factors such as passwords, one-time codes sent via text or email messages, biometrics like facial recognition, or fingerprints, depending on the sensitivity of data being accessed. For instance, financial transactions may require several identity verification tiers before approval, while less sensitive operations may not require stringent requirements. It is essential to establish authorization such that users are only granted access to specific features within an IA system by their role within the organization; this serves as a protective measure against accidental or deliberate misuse of data and systems by people who do not possess permission for certain activities. Encryption methods should protect confidential information from unauthorized access during network transfers (or between distinct locations).

Encryption can also be utilized as an additional layer of protection when storing data locally in databases or sending it over public networks such as WiFi hotspots. Moreover, conducting routine security audits and penetration testing will reveal any vulnerabilities within the system; this way, they may be quickly fixed before malicious entities can cause harm by exploiting these weaknesses. Such evaluations should occur at least once per annum; however, based on the risk profile associated with your environment – for example, if you manage large amounts of consumer information - more frequent tests could prove beneficial due to their elevated sensitivity.

Compliance and Regulations

Organizations of the present are faced with an unprecedented demand for managing security and risk related to their information technology systems. Therefore, there is a rising focus on the necessity of compliance and regulations in safeguarding sensitive data. Compliance and regulations are fundamental to any successful Information Assurance (IA) implementation strategy. They help guarantee that organizations comply with industry-standard IA protocols while reducing potential liabilities due to non-compliance or negligence.

The scope of required compliance may differ substantially depending on the type of operations conducted by the said organization, its geographic location, and pertinent federal and state laws.

Organizations must comprehend their lawful obligations to make sure they can suitably protect their data assets from unapproved access or misuse. Financial institutions must follow federal banking regulations, while healthcare providers must adhere strictly to HIPAA mandates concerning patient privacy rights. Adding more complexity is the ever-developing terrain of cyber threats, which necessitates organizations to stay alert in refreshing their defenses against novel attack vectors.

Organizations must establish comprehensive Information Assurance (IA) policies to comply with laws and regulations. These policies should cover authentication protocols, user privilege management, encryption technologies, patch management procedures, and incident response plans. Consequently, IT personnel familiar with the organization's specific compliance requirements should review these policies regularly to stay current, given changing business situations or technological developments over time. Employees must receive training regarding these policies to comprehend their obligations when upholding them uniformly across organizational operations. A frequent difficulty faced by many organizations is creating a practical compromise between operational safety measures required for compliance objectives while concurrently allowing users access to crucial systems and resources without significantly hindering overall system performance or productivity levels; this process takes up much-needed timing from other tasks which could potentially have more direct consequences upon organizational success indicators like customer satisfaction ratings or sales figures etcetera.

Training and Awareness

Regarding incorporating IA solutions, organizations must engage in appropriate security and risk management by deploying training and awareness programs. Training will equip employees with the knowledge required to identify risks related to their daily duties and how to act when presented with such threats. Moreover, initiatives centered around increasing employee understanding are necessary so new hires can stay informed of all existing safety protocols and industry standards. With effective programs like these put into practice, an organization stands a much better chance of minimizing its exposure level to potential hazards associated with AI implementation.

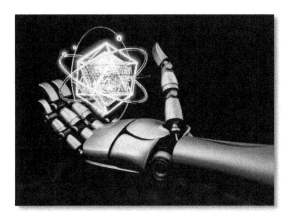

It is essential to create comprehensive training programs which cover every aspect of safety and risk control correlated with IA implementation. The program should incorporate topics such as discerning signals of a possible attack or break-in, comprehending data classification levels, designating roles for each team member included in establishing the system, responding suitably during an event occurrence, recognizing any third-party service providers employed for data processing or storage purposes and understanding regulatory necessities concerning data privacy or safeguard laws.

Organizations must develop awareness initiatives highlighting the importance of safeguarding their systems constantly. It should include providing employees with information regarding widespread dangers such as malware assaults or phishing emails and educating them on how to respond if confronted with a dubious activity or an attempted breach from external sources. Employees must also be aware of any internal policies related to safely utilizing organizational computers that will help diminish the potentiality of a successful attack being perpetrated against the organization's data assets by someone within its walls.

Moreover, it is critical that enterprises routinely inspect their security protocols concerning IA implementations so that they remain up-to-date with contemporary industry standards and best practices intended to protect confidential information resources from cyber threats, regardless of whether these attacks have been derived internally or externally. It is similarly imperative for companies o provide frequent notifications about transformations undertaken to enable staff members can stay informed about what actions need completing if something goes awry during the implementation process.

Future Trends in IA Security

As the world continues to evolve and advance technologically, there is a concurrent increase in demand for intelligent automation (IA) solutions that will allow organizations to improve their efficiency while reducing costs while meeting customer needs. Nonetheless, this swift growth of IA implementation leads to an elevated risk of cyber-attacks and data breaches, which must be addressed before any issues arise. Thus, companies must familiarize themselves with current trends related to IA security so they can take proper measures to safeguard against potential risks.

Organizations are presently facing one of the most significant difficulties in protecting their data from internal threats, such as malicious actors or those employees who have access to sensitive information yet need ample instruction to handle it securely. Organizations should be aware of measures relating to access control, like role-based access control (RBAC), which allows administrators to set particular authorizations for each user account based on their job functionality or degree of reliability within the organization. Additionally, instituting automated monitoring tools can detect peculiar activity quickly and apprise administrators when required so that any potential attack may be prevented straight away.

An additional significant trend that is becoming evident in the area of IA security is AI-driven threat detection systems. These use complex algorithms to detect potentially dangerous activity before it occurs. By utilizing machine learning models, these techniques can scan substantial amounts of information from multiple sources and recognize constructive which could result in a breach if ignored. Moreover, using an AI-driven system also offers continuous tracking for network changes so organizations can always stay ahead of potential attackers. Furthermore, biometric authentication methods have become increasingly common among corporations wanting extra protection against attempts at gaining access illegally by external parties or unscrupulous insiders inside an organization's network infrastructure itself. Biometrics requires users to offer corroborative evidence beyond usual username and password combinations via exclusive bodily attributes like fingerprints or facial scans, which cannot be imitated by someone wishing to gain unauthorized entry into a program. It makes biometrics particularly appealing when used with other identity verification processes, such as two-factor authentication (2FA).

Conclusion

Implementing Information Assurance Security and Risk Management is crucial for decreasing cyber threats and guaranteeing successful IA Implementation. Establishing an all-encompassing security strategy, recognizing risks, and having a reliable risk management plan are fundamental for prosperous IA execution. Organizations must be conscious of potential dangers to their framework, data, and applications to protect themselves from cyber assaults efficiently. Organizations can ensure that their IA Implementation endeavors are secure and productive by taking the essential steps to evaluate risks, construct strategies for hazard moderation, and deploy preventive measures.

Chapter 9

Ensuring Ethical Use of Gen AI in Government

The rise of technology has been a critical advantage for governments globally. But, with the emergence of new technologies like Artificial Intelligence (AI), ethical complications must be considered. Governments need to make sure they are employing AI ethically and conscientiously to provide better services to their citizens while also sidestepping any negative repercussions it may bring. Gen AI is an area within AI that focuses on creating systems able sensibility decide autonomously - obviously, this carries immense moral implications concerning government affairs too.

Understanding Generative AI and Its Potential in Government

Generative AI, or Generative Adversarial Networks (GANs), is a fantastic form of artificial intelligence with the potential to revolutionize many aspects of government operations. GANs can generate new data sets, find patterns in given data, automate tasks within governmental departments, and create novel ways to visualize complex issues. This type has potential applications across business and industry, and governments could also employ it - think of virtual simulations for policymaking or gain a clearer insight into how citizens feel about particular matters.

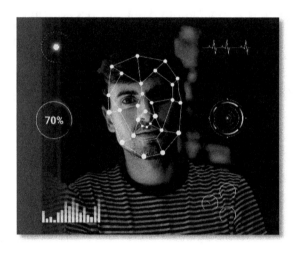

Using generative AI for government operations can be a double-edged sword. On the one hand, it could provide valuable insights into complex situations and help governments make more informed decisions. But on the other hand, without proper safeguards, there is an increased risk that biased or automated decision-making based on incorrect data sets or algorithms with unintended consequences might occur. What's more concerning - such decisions may even have severe implications, so how do we ensure that doesn't happen?

It is imperative to take proactive steps such as establishing explicit regulations concerning its usage and frequently evaluating the output results so any bias or errors are recognized in the early stages before influencing policy outcomes.

Additionally, ensuring all stakeholders' participation throughout the process - from crafting initial models through training them with proper datasets until keeping track of their performance over time when released into operation - is extremely important to utilize GANs properly. It will guarantee transparency during this entire procedure so that potential mistakes can be instantly identified and corrected if necessary while preventing improper utilization of general AI technology by malicious individuals who may have evil intent regarding a specific population group or political faction because there was no surveillance at the development phases.

Ethical Principles for Government Use of Gen AI

The ethical implications of using general AI in government are significant and must be considered. Since the emergence of this technology, many have wrestled with its potential misuse when it comes to governmental use - so specific rules must be followed for proper implementation. There must be a set framework underpinning these principles for consideration. How can we make sure what is put into place works as intended? What checks should happen if things don't go as planned, or how do we prevent such events? These questions need serious thought going forward so that general AI remains a safe technological direction both now and in the future.

First and foremost, when using general AI by any government, the safety and security of its citizens should always come first. They must work hard to ensure their privacy is not violated or misused - whether from within the government itself or even third parties who could potentially get access to data gathered through utilizing these systems. It's essential for people to have control over how their personal information is accessed, used, and saved if governments are planning on implementing such technology; this way, we all can feel secure knowing our sensitive details won't be taken advantage of without permission.

Second, when it comes to utilizing general AI-based systems for decision-making processes within a government body, transparency must be maintained throughout the entire process; not only should citizens have access to information about how decisions were made but also why certain decisions were made. Moreover, this technology must guarantee fairness and impartiality, which calls for regular evaluations and competent people trained in bias detection auditing them on accuracy grounds. This kind of technology will form an integral part of our society, so proper regulations are necessary before implementation begins - making sure everyone who takes part in using such a system understands what they can expect from deploying such a tool along with its responsibilities like personnel training or identifying areas where more research needs to be done ahead safely and ethically. Are we ready?

Potential Ethical Risks and Concerns

Ensuring ethical implementation of gen AI in governments is a demanding yet essential mission. Governments must be able to exploit the capabilities of Artificial Intelligence (AI) and associated technology while considering any potential ethical issues and concerns related to its use. The capacity for misuse or inappropriate utilization of AI tech has been well documented. Therefore, administrations must protect citizens from unethical applications this burgeoning technology might bring forth. One essential worry circling the virtuous employments of gen AI in government relates to data privacy - how can we ensure our personal information stays secure? What safety precautions must be taken not to compromise an individual's right to private life? These questions need immediate attention when attempting responsible implementations of artificial intelligence technologies within governmental structures.

As more government departments use AI-driven systems, they will require access to vast datasets containing citizens' details. This data can be utilized for various purposes, from helping deliver public services to understanding how policies affect different communities. However, governments must ensure that these databases remain safe and are only used in the intended manner. But what kind of measures should be taken? How secure is it behind the scenes - Are we sure our information remains confidential? Governmental agencies must work hard toward keeping this vital information out of the wrong hands.

Regarding data usage by governments, robust security protocols are essential for ensuring privacy. Using anonymized data is one such way to ensure the safety and protection of citizens' personal information. Governments should also be transparent about how this type of data is collected, stored, and used going forward - providing clarity on what happens to individual details when shared with governmental bodies.

Algorithmic bias presents a severe issue in regulations like these; algorithms created by humans may contain inherent biases due to pre-existing prejudices or limited datasets, which could lead them to treat certain groups unfairly or even provide inaccurate predictions – something decision-makers must avoid at all costs. There need to be more diverse teams developing government algorithms to not introduce built-in biases into them from the outset – a critical consideration given their widespread production environment deployments without proper oversight mechanisms in place." Moreover, rigorous testing before deployment would help catch any unforeseen problems resulting from algorithmic bias before those consequences become real-world ones later - protecting users who ultimately rely upon accurate models being put out there.

Implementing Ethical AI Audits and Impact Assessments

AI technology is developing rapidly and changing the world in ways we could have never foreseen. Governments around the globe are increasingly implementing AI-based solutions to be more efficient, cut costs, and provide better services for citizens. Nevertheless, as AI becomes integral to government operations, governments must use ethical approaches to apply this technology. To guarantee this happens, conducting ethical audits and impact assessments can help governments anticipate consequences for people or other parties before introducing new policies or systems dependent on artificial intelligence implementations. **How will these changes affect us? What kind of effects should we prepare ourselves for in our day-to-day lives?**

We must ensure that the AI systems used by governments adhere to specific fairness, transparency, and accountability standards while designing, implementing, and operating. An ethical audit can help identify potential risks like bias or discrimination in these decisions, which might negatively affect individuals. Moreover, impact assessment allows us to evaluate the effects of proposed policies on different stakeholders before implementation so we can make informed choices regarding deployment of them at all or not.

Government organizations must create robust moral frameworks when they launch new technologies such as Artificial Intelligence (AI). If there are no proper regulations set up beforehand, then it will likely produce unanticipated biases within their rules resulting in unjust outcomes for citizens influenced by them.

International Collaboration and Governance

Collaboration on a global scale is essential for the ethical use of general AI in government operations. Nations must come together and build one universal set of regulations, rules that could be used across countries with different cultures and languages. By taking united action, governments can create policies that will reduce the risks posed by new technologies while considering local needs. It's wise for governments to form an international body or commission responsible for setting global standards when using gen AI in government-related activities.

Creating an expert body of multiple disciplines like computer science, law enforcement, public policy experts, sociologists, economists, and ethicists within and outside the government is essential. This commission should be independently mandated with the authority to review present laws on gen AI usage in governmental applications and provide guidance for secure deployment. Legislative bodies can use its findings when framing local regulations regarding gen AI utilization. Cooperation amongst countries needs particular attention since divergent approaches between nations would cause havoc once advances are made internationally or across several states at a time. Furthermore, collaboration allows resource sharing that leads swiftly towards finding solutions, such as deciding suitable data collection methods while training algorithms or crafting systems made explicitly for privacy protection imprints during gen AI technology's application by governments.

Conclusion

Governments must ensure the ethical use of Gen AI to keep their people safe and maintain the trust given. Governments should create legislation enforcing proper behavior when using artificial intelligence technology to ensure this happens. Additionally, government agencies should value both outside expertise from the public and private sectors as they develop regulations and guidelines for ethically handling Gen AI tech – which is essential for ensuring no misuse occurs at any point during its application or operation.

Chapter 10

Integrating IA with Legacy Government Systems

T he government always strives to make its systems more efficient and effective, so they've been looking into ways to do this. Enter artificial intelligence (AI). AI has the potential to revolutionize the way governments operate by automating processes, reducing costs, and consolidating data - all at once. We will study how integrating AI into legacy government systems can improve them while discussing any challenges that come with it. We'll look at the automation of processes and data consolidation strategies that could prove beneficial when using artificial intelligence in these situations - what kind of impact will such an implementation have? Ultimately we hope to provide insight into how incorporating AI into existing governmental technology may be just the thing needed for a significant transformation.

Understanding IA Legacy Government Systems

Integrating AI with legacy government systems can be a challenging endeavor. As technology advances, it is necessary to incorporate modern Artificial Intelligence (AI) capabilities into existing government structures. Knowing how these older systems work is essential to achieve successful integration. Legacy government systems are those that have been present for an extended period and are usually based on out-of-date technologies, which makes them complicated to adjust to the current expectations.

Taking on Artificial Intelligence (AI) as part of a legacy system is a big undertaking. It's essential to begin assessing what is already in place and ascertain where AI can be best utilized for increased efficiency or accuracy. It requires gaining insight into how data is structured, stored and any potential security risks that could come up when using this technology. Once these areas have been identified, setting down the correct strategy for inserting AI capabilities within the current system will become your top priority.

Integrating AI technology with legacy government systems can be tricky and challenging. It requires experts' help to ensure all components work harmoniously or even create custom solutions for meeting the organization's mission objectives. There may also be compatibility issues between new applications and existing members in older systems that must be addressed before successful implementation. For instance, if an organization's software doesn't support certain data types needed by an AI application, then extra resources need to go into finding compatible solutions or upgrading the infrastructure before launching initiatives involving the integration of AI technology. In other words, it is essential for teams wanting to incorporate these technologies into their operations to consider carefully any potential obstacles they could face along the way - especially those related to system compatibility.

Challenges of Integration

Integrating AI with legacy government systems can be a tough nut to crack. Over the years, governments have heavily invested in these outdated and inefficient legacy systems - which are not only technologically obsolete but also lack up-to-date security protocols for integrating modern technologies such as AI. These issues manifest themselves when attempting to integrate IA into existing governmental operations since many of these older systems aren't explicitly engineered, keeping integration requirements in consideration.

The architecture and design of the system may be decades-old, making it challenging to integrate modern technologies like AI or machine learning algorithms. It can pose a significant issue as considerable time and resources are needed for changes to be made to accommodate these new technologies. And while this could prove beneficial in the long run, it's undeniable that such investments come at a cost - both monetary and temporal. How effectively would you use your limited budget if presented with this task?

Integrating AI and other new technologies into older government systems takes a lot of work. There are a lot of complexities surrounding them, so understanding how they work can be challenging for developers - making it difficult to avoid unforeseen issues or conflicts during the process. Furthermore, integrating AI with existing processes requires comprehensive data management as well. It means collecting information from various sources within an organization; moreover, this info must cross-check external datasets to guarantee accuracy and reliability when decisions are made based on these analyses. Plus, there are privacy regulations that must be respected, too - created by local governments, which add another layer of complexity since changes made could potentially conflict with current laws already established by certain jurisdictions worldwide. All considered, good progress is being made toward successful integration, but more development work must be done before we reach satisfactory results.

Strategies for Integration

Legacy government systems have been around for a while, and even though they may work well in specific ways, it can take time to integrate them with modern tech. Thankfully, some tactics could help us make integrating these more accessible and practical. The first step is ensuring all the systems involved play nice together - data formats must match up properly to recover information during the transition. It's critical to double-check everything before moving forward here.

Integrating legacy government systems with intelligent automation (IA) solutions can be confusing and challenging. It's essential to take specific steps before initiating such projects - ensuring the hardware used by existing systems is still supported in current software versions. Taking these precautions ahead of time will help reduce any issues during integration attempts.

A great strategy when attempting system integrations like this one is to approach them incrementally; beginning small and gradually expanding as successes are achieved along the way allows you to identify problems early on so that your team may adjust their methods accordingly rather than finding out about complications later after taking up more resources on a larger-scale project. Breaking apart tasks into smaller parts also makes them more straightforward for staff members who might not have usable knowledge surrounding IA or specific elements from legacy frameworks – giving everyone involved enough opportunity to become comfortable working through each portion of an assignment before moving onto something else.

Lastly, anyone tackling such endeavors must know both sides if they expect reliable results: detail-oriented comprehension of IA technology and components within old governmental infrastructure should always come first.

How do experts go about combining different pieces? What technical capabilities does my organization possess which would allow us smooth transitions? Questions like those could provide valuable insight toward understanding successful integrations throughout institutions or organizations

IA Applications in Government

Many industries have rapidly embraced Artificial Intelligence (AI), which is becoming a critical feature of present-day business. While private companies have implemented AI without hesitation, governments took their time - but lately, there have been some notable progressions in using this technology within governmental structures. This integration might bring many benefits to administrations, such as improved public service delivery and saving money and time, which certainly can't be overlooked.

However, when introducing Artificial Intelligence to official government systems, we are faced with quite an issue - how do we ensure that our cutting-edge tech works appropriately with existing legacy technology?

Legacy systems can be complicated, and integrating them with new technologies takes work. For this reason, ensuring that AI solutions are compatible with existing infrastructure is critical. With the proper integration, these solutions bring plenty of benefits for government operations - like amplified efficiency and effectiveness when making decisions or better access to data analytics opportunities. Moreover, such integration opens up ways of collaboration between different departments within the government and external stakeholders, allowing everyone involved to combine old-school technology with modern approaches while also coming up with creative ideas on how to solve problems using both simultaneously. Sounds too good? Maybe – but why don't we give it a try?

When introducing AI systems into the government's legacy architecture, several security risks and protocols must be taken to guard against cyber threats or data leakage. Besides, governments planning on implementing IA solutions within their organization should thoroughly comprehend all the potential risks involved before taking any further steps; this includes ensuring they have the right people with sufficient knowledge of technical matters from the implementation stage through the maintenance period if necessary.

Despite these obstacles, however, more and more countries around the globe have started acknowledging how valuable an efficient integration of IA applications could bring - both economically and profit-wise - when appropriately done inside their existing system structure.

Data Security and Privacy

Data security and privacy have become a massive worry for governments worldwide as they look to integrate AI with their existing government systems. Integrating AI could revolutionize how these organizations make decisions. Still, it also brings up plenty of data safety issues that must be addressed before the integration can occur properly. Governments must ensure any new AI system is secure and follows all applicable data protection laws- including GDPR, HIPAA, or anything else relevant. It calls for serious consideration of current laws regarding subjects like this one.

Making sure our government uses AI responsibly requires a two-tiered approach. First, organizations must deploy secure protocols for data security. It means developing strong internal practices that involve encryption techniques and access control systems to keep data safe from unauthorized users. Next, governments should protect their citizens' privacy when interacting with AI programs by incorporating safeguards into automated decision-making processes such as audits—ensuring the accuracy of the information they use without bias or unfair treatment towards certain people or groups. Additionally, there needs to be clear communication around how personal info is gathered and used so all involved understand their power over accessing and deleting it. It's essential to work closely with specialists both specialized in cyber defense AND artificial intelligence who can provide invaluable input on proper methods for protecting public safety along with private citizen information when introducing advanced computer technologies into government operations.

Conclusion

Incorporating Artificial Intelligence (AI) into existing government systems can be incredibly beneficial. Automating processes and data consolidation will improve accuracy, streamline efficiency and reduce costs in the long run. AI is an essential tool to maximize data management and analyze evidence-based decisions - this ultimately leads to increased operational efficiency for government authorities, which contributes positively to their overall performance. Engaging with AI technology could benefit organizations today; it provides them with helpful information that they may not have access to otherwise, which enables better decision-making at a faster rate.

Chapter 11

Best Practices for Intelligent Automation in Government

The government's capacity to grapple with complicated issues and respond swiftly to ever-changing needs depends on its ability to adapt intelligent automation. By following the right strategies and practices, governments can use automation to heighten efficiency, lower costs, and improve service delivery.

Importance of intelligent automation for government efficiency

Undoubtedly, the government sector is under immense pressure to provide efficient and effective services at a reduced cost. Intelligent automation has emerged as a crucial agent in helping governments improve their processes and operations. It involves using software or robotics process automation (RPA) technology to automate tasks, streamline workflows and better understand how the government functions. It can be highly advantageous for organizations looking for ways to maximize their resources while minimizing costs – but are there risks associated?

Making use of intelligent automation can bring a slew of benefits to governments. It could reduce the manual labor associated with administrative tasks while optimizing resource utilization. It, in turn, translates into improved customer service and engagement for citizens as well operational efficiency and accuracy throughout government agencies. Automating compliance-related tasks such as document management and audit tracking/reporting would also minimize redundancies regarding data entry or processing activities. So how will all this benefit the citizens? Well, wait times are reduced, and access to information is made available quicker.

Take, for example, automated chatbots. It's a great way to provide customer service, cutting out wait times that usually occur due to human response time restrictions. This same concept can be applied to public record searches - eliminating the need for an in-person intermediary and saving both parties precious time.

Intelligent automation goes even further than this, though, with its ability to automate rule-based tasks like document routing or application processing according to set parameters or regulations -- leading toward improved regulation compliance across all departments within an agency.

Benefits of Intelligent Automation in Government

Intelligent automation is becoming increasingly popular in government operations. It's a great way to improve efficiency and reduce costs. It significantly benefits governments because it can directly influence the quality of public services they deliver. For instance, many countries are utilizing intelligent automation to speed up immigration application processing and improve customer service for citizens who want access to government services. It makes getting these vital processes done faster and with greater ease than ever before - imagine how much more efficient things would be if every area had this technology!

Automating tasks such as document scans, background checks, and identity verifications can get applicants more rapid responses from government offices. It saves time and reduces errors caused by manual processing procedures. Through intelligent automation in the public sector, decision-making processes within an organization are improved too! Automation of data entry and analysis frees up the resources needed to do these functions manually; otherwise - it's a win-win situation! With this move towards technological advancement, customers will receive better services with fewer issues related to application status or response times arising due lack of staff or mistakes made during paperwork. Intelligent automation provides us many advantages; It helps organizations run while simultaneously ensuring excellent customer satisfaction – saving everybody's precious time.

By automating mundane administrative tasks, personnel can be freed up to focus on more complex problem-solving or policy decisions. This approach allows an organization to make better-informed decisions based on comprehensive data sets rather than relying solely on anecdotal evidence and human judgment. Ultimately, this improves governance as the decision-making process is rooted in reliable information rather than guesswork. With that being said, could utilizing technology help you streamline specific processes and create a system of stronger oversight?

Ultimately, intelligent automation can help government operations become more cost-effective. It is because manual labor costs associated with specific processes or functions are eliminated when these tasks have been automated instead of done manually. Automation also lowers the likelihood of mistakes due to human error, which could result in expensive fines being incurred by an organization if not rectified quickly. All this means that expenses for all departments can be reduced, resulting in better fiscal responsibility and more significant savings overall. It's incredible how much impact AI-based technology has on our daily lives - even what one might think as a mundane process, such as running a governmental operation, proves beneficial from utilizing automation.

Critical Use Cases in Government Intelligent Automation

Government Intelligent Automation has many perks, including cost savings, better services, and an improved citizen experience. By introducing automation into government operations, it is possible to reduce manual labor costs, increase accuracy and improve the efficiency of proceedings. Thanks to intelligent automation, the government can enhance its processes by streamlining document processing or data entry, automating customer service using chatbots, and optimizing back-office functions such as accounts payable with A.I. technology that allows decisions based on real-time analysis. Document processing deserves special attention when using intelligence automation since various departments in the public sector may benefit from its optimization capabilities for workflow purposes. What's more - this clever solution doesn't just save time but also helps organizations be more effective at delivering value through optimized processes.

Automating document processes has several benefits. It helps digitize documents to cut down on paper waste. It sends them straight to the right place for approval or rejection while simultaneously extracting relevant information from them and storing it digitally. It saves time previously spent manually entering data into various systems, reduces errors due to manual inputting of numbers or words, and decreases physical space needed for filing away hard copies of paperwork since everything is now stored digitally - which also enhances security by having electronic versions instead.

Customer service can also be significantly improved through intelligent automation; chatbots allow governments to respond quickly without requiring human interaction 24/7. So citizens' inquiries can be answered almost immediately with no need for someone sitting behind a desk all day waiting to help – how great would that be?

Chatbots can be an excellent way to give personalized results in an automated manner and ensure citizens get their questions answered promptly, no matter what time of the day or night. When you have large amounts of customer inquiries, like tax filing or housing help during peak times when human resources might not be available because of holidays or other reasons that are out of anyone's hands -

chatbots can serve as great front-line responders. On top of that, Intelligent Automation allows governments to streamline back office procedures such as accounts payable with automated workflows, guaranteeing accuracy while cutting down on labor costs associated with those processes. How sweet is that?

Best Practices for Implementing Intelligent Automation in Government

Implementing intelligent automation in government is becoming increasingly essential for keeping up with citizens' growing demands and the needs of the public sector. Governments around the globe are utilizing various forms of automated technology like robotic process automation (RPA), artificial intelligence (A.I.), and machine learning (ML) to better processes, lower costs, increase proficiency, and eliminate mistakes while offering quality services to their people. But integrating intelligent automation can be difficult due to factors such as rules/regulations, budget limitations, or data privacy issues, among other matters. The question here is; how do governments effectively use AI-driven technologies?

Governments must grasp the best practices to implement intelligent automation successfully. The first step is deciding which processes can benefit from being automated; there needs to be enough data available so A.I./ML-based models or robotics process automation tools can function correctly. If that criterion is met, those processes become priority candidates for using I.A. technology – a big decision!

Everybody involved in the project must be up for using new technologies before initiating any implementation. Who are we talking about here? The process owners. They will be managing automated tasks or activities once they have been set up correctly, and these guys need to give the green light beforehand so everything can go as planned.

It includes understanding when human intervention will still be necessary within specific tasks or activities during an automated workflow and knowing how decision-making capabilities can interact with existing laws & regulations while using AI/ML models. A secure I.T. infrastructure must also be set up to guarantee data protection for sensitive information that may pass through government systems and networks while undergoing various automated workflows.

After implementing intelligent automation solutions, governments need to keep tracking performance levels to spot potential improvements or optimizations that could further increase the benefits of these technologies across different departments or agencies within their organization. By following good practices, governments worldwide can ensure successful implementations of Intelligent Automation technology in their operations resulting in high service delivery standards at decreased costs and improved efficiency throughout public organizations.

Usage of Intelligent Automation in U.S. Government

Gaining traction in the U.S. government, Intelligent Automation (I.A.) is not an unexpected trend. I.A. provides governments with a whole host of perks, such as enhanced efficiency, heightened accuracy, and cost-cutting benefits - making it essential for governments to implement best practices when integrating automation into operations. Before further down this route, however, organizations must get acquainted with their systems and processes; foresight here is crucial to maximizing these advantages.

Understanding how current processes work and where they could be improved is the key to identifying which areas Artificial Intelligence (A.I.) can best be used. A plan outlining how A.I. will be implemented into existing operations is essential; this should include objectives that determine what tasks need to be automated first and the type of automation intended for each job. It's also crucial to remember resource availability when implementing A.I.; government departments must have adequate resources if the successful implementation of A.I. within their operations is desired.

It is essential for organizations wanting to use intelligent automation solutions that they have a team of personnel knowledgeable in A.I. and experienced in designing effective processes with an emphasis on automated integration points between different systems or functions within the department/agency. On top of this, teams need to be able to maintain all necessary records related to their electronic execution so performance over time can be accurately monitored when required by law or regulation. Risk management around implementing such technology needs careful consideration – data security issues, privacy concerns, etc. - should always ensure the safety & protection of citizens of data. To help strategies here, governments must remain up-to-date with current laws, regulations, standards, policies, procedures best practices regarding the development & deployment intelligent of intelligent automation as well as other pertinent information, specifically toward risk management.

Conclusion

Intelligent automation has the potential to be utilized by governments in an effective manner which can lead to increased efficiency and improved outcomes for citizens. Government entities must take specific steps towards using this technology at their best capacity. It includes aligning automated processes with existing structures understanding associated risks, and implementing sound governance models. By doing so, governments can leverage intelligent automation to bring about positive change within operations while delivering better services for taxpayers - all of which are tremendous opportunities.

Chapter 12

Case Studies of I.A. and Gen AI Adoption in Governments

It's no shock that governments worldwide are turning to Artificial Intelligence (A.I.) and General AI (Gen AI) to streamline operations. We will study numerous case studies of I.A. and Gen AI usage within various jurisdictions, from small local authorities to expansive federal administrations.

I.A. and General AI Adoption in U.S. Federal Government:

The U.S. Federal Government has been investigating the advantages of A.I. and I.A. (Intelligent Automation) technologies - their potential for improved efficiency, accuracy, and cost savings across its multiple departments. Recently quite a few agencies have taken the initiative to incorporate these bleeding-edge techniques in their procedures. Let's look at some significant case studies reflecting I.A. & general Artificial Intelligence implementation within government entities such as the Department of Defense (DoD), the National Institutes of Health (NIH),& U.S. Postal Service (USPS). How are they using this knowledge? What results can be expected from it? These questions should spark our curiosity.

The Department of Defense is utilizing Artificial Intelligence algorithms to automate logistics management, supply chain management, personnel/training handling, and budget activities in their operations centers all across the globe. These systems are meant to improve precision and reduce costs linked with human labor while also bringing increased situational awareness for decision-makers on a battlefield or when dealing with strategic plans such as finances or logistical planning. What kind of results can this A.I. get? Can it slash expenses associated with manual work? That remains yet to be seen.

The Department of Defense has developed applications for predictive maintenance to be used by service members on military equipment such as planes and vehicles. It is aimed at helping them keep things operational in a wartime situation; this hardware needs regular upkeep if it remains combat-ready. What kind of battles will our troops face? And how can we equip them with the tools they need to be prepared no matter what comes their way?

These apps provide one possible solution - though obviously, there are many more out there too.

At the National Institutes of Health (NIH), researchers are finding many ways to use machine learning models for biomedical research analysis. For instance, pharmaceutical companies around the world leverage these tools in drug discovery and development processes; image recognition algorithms help identify diagnostic features within medical images; natural language processing assists with text mining from scientific publications; bioinformatics solutions integrate genetics data from different sources into a single platform; robots enable scientists to conduct experiments more quickly and efficiently than ever before while automated systems assist with study design. The possibilities that come along with leveraging ML technology in healthcare science seem almost endless - NIH staff members rely on it every day!

182

Finally, USPS is introducing robotic process automation solutions into its mail sorting facilities across the United States. These places organize millions of pieces of mail each day before they reach their final destination. With these intelligent bots, postal workers can do tedious tasks faster than ever, and costs associated with manual labor are reduced considerably. On top of that, USPS also has leveraged machine learning algorithms applied to customer databases to find behavioral patterns which measure customers' satisfaction levels when using services provided by employees or detect any potential frauds related to credit card information, among other similar cases - an incredible use for technology.

State-Level IA and General AI Adoption: California: Texas

California and Texas are two states that stand out when it comes to the adoption of artificial intelligence (A.I.) and general AI in governments. Both have been at the forefront, taking advantage of this technology for their services and operations.

In California, they've taken several initiatives, including using A.I. for predictive analytics, natural language processing, facial recognition - even autonomous vehicle testing! It's incredible how far these tools can take government efficiency today; who would have thought such sophisticated technologies could have been employed just a decade ago?

In Texas, Governor Greg Abbott is taking a huge step to make the state an A.I. hub. He has invested $3 million in university research grants to further its development. Not only this, but his office also established a task force on artificial intelligence that aims to find ways of using this technology so that the government can improve its services and provide better efficiency for citizens - how cool.

We're looking forward to seeing what new initiatives will come from these investments.

California and Texas have implemented policies to promote innovation in the A.I. field with tax credits for companies developing such tech solutions and incentives for researchers looking into how A.I. can be used more effectively within government functions.

Moreover, they are mindful of potential issues surrounding this technology, like privacy concerns or algorithm bias that could lead to unequal treatment based on specific characteristics. To combat these obstacles, they have set up organizations dedicated to legal oversight, like California's

Office of Artificial Intelligence Ethics, which will keep tabs on compliance with pertinent laws regarding using data collected from citizens or businesses through their technologies.

Both states are taking steps forward by utilizing artificial intelligence-based techniques, which should help increase efficiency while keeping a watchful eye out. Hence, no misuse occurs down the line - ensuring any negative consequences don't arise from wrongful power usage from day one.

Challenges of I.A. and Gen AI Usage in the U.S. Federal Government

The U.S. federal government has undoubtedly witnessed the challenges of incorporating Artificial Intelligence (A.I.) and General AI (Gen AI). With a complex yet ever-evolving legal landscape, embracing modern technology brings unique difficulties for the authorities. Numerous obstacles must be addressed, from privacy issues to ethical matters, before any successful adaption. One of the most daunting tasks confronting this sector is finding secure ways to store and manage all data involved when harnessing I.A. plus Gen AI - How exactly do government departments ensure their precious information remains safe?

Managing the vast amounts of personal and confidential information collected by agencies is no small feat. They must ensure this data stays secure and that personnel can access it based on their roles. It's complicated stuff.

A challenge U.S. federal agencies face when incorporating I.A. and Gen AI technologies is how to make the most out of these resources so that changes across their operations or services are meaningful. Yet, high standards in terms of quality and accuracy remain.

Local Government Initiatives in the USA

The U.S. government has recently made great strides in utilizing A.I. and I.A. technology. A notable local project implemented is the City of San Francisco's Smart City Initiative, which started in 2018. This attempt focused on using data and technology to make everyday living better for citizens with improved transportation systems, energy conservation, public safety, and more. With a vision to accomplish this goal, the city elected an IBM Watson partnership to create an AI-powered platform accessible by anyone in real time - providing information about traffic patterns, crime rates, and weather forecasts just like that!

The system in Los Angeles also utilizes predictive analytics to give citizens a heads-up about potential perils and risks near them. This plan has been successful so far, as it lessens the crime rate while at the same time giving emergency services quicker reaction times; all this with the added benefit of providing people access to relevant information which they usually wouldn't have had.

In 2019, L.A. initiated its own Local Government Innovation Program (LGIP). Its primary purpose is to promote inventive solutions that tackle serious matters such as poverty minimization, homeless prevention, and health improvements.

The program assists entrepreneurs to link up with local government resources to turn their ideas into valuable products or services that will make Los Angeles residents' lives healthier while helping businesses grow sustainably. LGIP has several initiatives, such as its Civic Innovation Challenge grants program, providing funding for outstanding projects related to civic participation solutions using AI/IA technology and taking the lead on how cities effectively use tech innovations for social good at a town level over numerous domains like healthcare delivery systems and housing management programs similar those already implemented by some cities like Seattle WA who are utilizing machine learning algorithms on rental applications together with background checks of applicants resulting in better outputs than traditional methods previously available when these technologies weren't around yet.

Future Trends and Considerations

As technology constantly develops, government agencies should be prepared to take on the changes that come with it. With AI and General AI gradually becoming more visible in public sector operations, administrations must consider adapting these new technologies to their day-to-day activities.

When analyzing future trends for incorporating A.I. in governments, two significant aspects have to be looked at: practicality and cost-effectiveness. Governments need to ensure any solutions they implement can scale up or down depending on the organization's needs."

Governments need to explore solutions that give a long-term return on investment. It could involve using cloud models or open-source options whenever possible. They also need to consider how A.I. can be employed responsibly in their establishments while recognizing its ethical problems, such as data secrecy and algorithmic prejudice. Governments must attempt to make rules and regulations that permit them to apply A.I. morally while simultaneously preserving people's privileges and liberties. To stay up-to-date with existing developments in the adoption of A.I. technology, governments should look into participating in industry events/conferences associated with this subject, reading case studies from other public sector organizations who have executed similar systems, teaming up with external associates like universities or private companies; or doing experimental projects related new technologies including robotics and natural language processing (NLP). What do all these things entail? That is why policymakers need another perspective - an outside view.

Conclusion

Governments must be mindful and conscious of the implications of A.I. and Gen AI adoption on their policies. They must take into account the potential outcomes before moving forward. Doing so ensures that citizens receive better services while promptly meeting legal obligations. Governments should weigh all options before implementing any new technology; by doing this, everyone benefits from an improved quality of life.

Chapter 13

Future Outlook: Advancements and Opportunities

As we enter the 21st century, Artificial Intelligence (A.I.) and General AI (Gen AI) provide us with more opportunities than ever. With automation being made more accessible and better technology forecasts to help support this trend, these advances offer us almost endless possibilities. We can look at some potential benefits of advancing our use of both A.I.s and Gen-Ais in terms of opening up new opportunities for ourselves now and in the future. Moreover, what challenges may arise from leveraging such technologies? What would be their effect on society moving ahead?

Advancements in Intelligence Augmentation (I.A.)

As the tech world transforms, we see new possibilities for businesses and people due to intelligence augmentation (I.A.) and general artificial intelligence (Gen AI) developments. I.A. is a branch of computer science that focuses on boosting human cognitive abilities utilizing computers and other digital technologies. Conversely, Gen AI is an advanced form of Artificial Intelligence that can "think," study from its environment, and adjust according to different situations. It's anticipated that both types of cutting-edge technology will significantly affect our lifestyles in the coming years -What kind of impact could it bring? How might these changes influence us individually or collectively?

Businesses can benefit from I.A. by automating the dull and time-consuming tasks that employees usually do. This automation will save time and give businesses a better understanding of customer habits that could be used to inform future business decisions. Additionally, Gen AI has been able to take autonomous vehicles or robotic arms in industrial settings to new heights with its speed and accuracy

- something that wasn't ever thought possible before! Who knows what else these advancements can bring?

On an individual level, I.A. can help us become more productive and efficient by allowing us to complete complex tasks faster or more accurately than ever before. Meanwhile, Gen AI could provide a great boon for those who need assistance due to age or disability— granting them access to services that may not have been available without expensive hardware solutions or dedicated caregivers. Wondering what else this technology has in store? What other opportunities might arise from its use?

I.A. and Gen AI will make a huge difference in our lives professionally and personally. But of course, like with any new technology, there is an associated risk, so precautionary measures must be taken while developing these systems. Proper security protocols should consistently be implemented from the beginning to deployment; this helps keep data safe and malicious actors out of their codes.

If we handle its challenges smartly, though, we are on the cusp of a world where machines become actual extensions rather than tools for aiding us in daily life, something people have been contemplating ever since computing began.

What does this mean? Can anything truly replace human judgment? Are computer-run decisions more reliable than those made by humans?

Advancements in General Artificial Intelligence (Gen AI)

General Artificial Intelligence (Gen AI) improvements have been remarkable lately. As more and more businesses invest heavily in A.I. research, its sophistication has sky-rocketed, and it has the potential to revolutionize several different industries and applications. This cutting-edge technology is being utilized for automating numerous processes - from customer service to medical diagnosis - helping us speed up our workflows like never before! Moreover, Gen AI can aid in tackling the world's most complex challenges by giving insights into complicated data sets that would otherwise be impossible or too tough for humans to process effectively. When you think about it this way – isn't this incredible?

The possibilities that Gen AI presents for the future are unique. For instance, businesses can use it to provide better customer service by automating tedious tasks and giving people an efficient response when they make inquiries or complaints. Additionally, machine learning algorithms can be used in predictive analytics so companies can foretell what their customers want before anything happens - leading to more accurate decisions and, thus, higher sales figures or improved efficiency of operations.

On a personal level, we'd benefit from automated systems which can recognize patterns faster and accurately but still guarantee our privacy with advanced protocols such as blockchain technology; this could give us access to data much quicker than usual while also providing information about our environment which would otherwise not be available without something like Gen AI-enabled automation capabilities.

Opportunities of Intelligence Augmentation (I.A.) and General Artificial Intelligence (Gen AI)

Artificial Intelligence (AI's) potential is an exhilarating idea, promising to transform practically all industries. Even though A.I. has been around since the 1950s, it's only recently gained a lot of attention in many different fields. Generally speaking, there are two main types of A.I.: Intelligence Augmentation (I.A.) and General Artificial Intelligence (Gen AI). I.A. focuses on increasing human intelligence by providing individuals with improved skills. On the other hand, Gen AI mainly targets creating machines that can think and act like people - what does this mean for us humans?

The possibilities for both A.I. and General Artificial Intelligence are immense. For example, I.A. can be utilized by professionals to increase their mental capacities so they can make more intelligent choices or take more advantageous activities dependent on their setting or circumstance. Additionally, predictive analysis devices can help organizations make increasingly educated decisions regarding apportioning assets and managing operations more productively. What's incredible about this is that these systems don't just process data—they also learn from it.

Companies have access to better insights than ever before when making those critical business decisions, giving them an edge over competitors who may still need to be up-to-date with the latest developments in A.I. technology.

Gen AI and Artificial Intelligence are used for various applications as we move further into the A.I. world. For instance, with Natural Language Processing (NLP), customers can use voice activation to interact with companies. It would be a more efficient way of communication as it eliminates laborious manual tasks! Additionally, robots could perform complex procedures that require expertise or any human involvement, which is not always available; overall saving costs related to mundane processes while giving businesses an increase in productivity at the same time. Wouldn't it be great if machines handled all our tedious jobs?

Businesses can already use automated systems powered by machine learning algorithms for process automation, significantly saving time and money. Moreover, computer vision solutions based on deep learning technologies can be used for inventory management- reducing errors and increasing accuracy! The development of A.I. and General Artificial Intelligence will continue in line with technology's ever-accelerating growth rate - introducing even more exciting opportunities than those before it. For example, predictive analytics tools yield better decisions, while computer visions aid efficiency when managing stocks. Businesses everywhere have been reaping these benefits from such advancements, which they will likely experience long into the future.

Challenges and Considerations

The advancements in A.I. and Gen AI tech are happening quickly, with new daily developments. But we still need to consider the potential issues that come with these technologies before they can reach their actual heights. One of the biggest problems is that there needs to be a comprehensive strategy for using these tools correctly. Without a solid plan guiding us on what we should do regarding A.I. and Gen AIs, any usage carries its risks, which could be hard to predict or manage – so creating an agreed-upon approach would make a big difference here.

Also, there's an urgent need for more research to understand how these systems operate and interact together so that they're secure. It raises the problematic question concerning privacy rights when it comes to data collected by A.I. as well as Gen AI systems. As these technologies become increasingly powerful, they also start spying on our lives in a much bigger way - gathering all kinds of info about what we do, who we are, where we go, etc. So this raises legitimate concerns regarding people's right to personal information; with great power (A.I. & Gen apps) could also come severe threats if not monitored appropriately.

A.I. and Gen AI technology have a lot of potential applications. But with this kind of power comes the responsibility to use it responsibly - ensuring individuals' data is handled securely, creating laws protecting personal information, and understanding ethical implications before using such powerful tech for any purpose.

When it comes to data privacy, organizations utilizing advanced technologies should be held accountable by ensuring there are ways for people to maintain control over their information – like being able to review what types of info third parties can access about them or how long it's stored, etcetera. This way, everyone benefits: users get better security, while companies benefit from more user trust in exchange! On the other hand, if these protocols aren't followed, we could end up seeing disastrous results due to algorithmic bias leading certain chronically disadvantaged groups further away from accessing the services they need most. So given all this complexity, you just got to wonder: why take chances?

Future Pathways and Strategies

Artificial intelligence (A.I.) and general AI's future is ever-evolving. In the last few years, there have been massive improvements in both areas going from strength to strength with their capabilities increasing substantially. This technology offers businesses, governments, and individuals tremendous prospects, but it continues - we must prepare for what lies ahead too. We all know that advances in this space are happening quickly, so it's vital to keep up with them and stay one step ahead by exploring potential opportunities further down the line.

Understanding the current advances in Artificial Intelligence (A.I.) and Generative A.I. is insufficient. We need to identify potential strategies that could create a direction for these fields in years ahead, going beyond short-term goals towards more long-term objectives. To move into this new era, we must explore what pathways are available - one way or another, it's all about pushing forward with our ideas and concepts. It makes you wonder how we can be sure those approaches will work. What should they look like exactly? How do we go from where we are now to what is out there waiting for us in the future with A.I. technology?

Creating models that can self-learn could be a great strategy. Instead of relying on traditional algorithms with hardcoded instructions or training datasets, reinforcement learning techniques and unsupervised deep learning networks may build their decision trees from experience - giving us powerful machines able to handle complex tasks without needing human interaction all the time. It would have significant implications across healthcare, finance, and beyond! Additionally, exploring ways for machines to interact with humans using natural language processing rather than preprogrammed commands/responses is another avenue worth considering; this will provide greater insight into how people think while creating better user experiences through more intuitive machine interactions for end users. Soaking up real-life conversations between two people makes you realize how much nuance goes into communication - something we hope our technology will master one day.

Conclusion

A.I. advancement and Gen AI prospects have opened up a world of possibilities for the near future. Technological forecasts suggest that our use of intelligent automation will bring plenty of advantages across industries soon enough. It is essential to recognize these advancements and take full advantage of them to succeed better as a business in the future - what kind of opportunities can we uncover while leveraging this technology? What are the potential benefits for us if utilized correctly? With proper analysis, businesses can reap the rewards of understanding such new technologies.

References

- Smith, J. A. (2020). Understanding Intelligent Automation: Concepts and Applications. Academic Press.
- Johnson, M. B. (2019). Generative AI: State of the Art and Future Directions. Journal of Artificial Intelligence Research, 65, 863-889.
- OECD. (2018). Going Digital: Making the Transformation Work for Growth and Well-being. Organization for Economic Co-operation and Development.
- Kamar, E., Horvitz, E., & Ramchurn, S. (2020). Benefits and Challenges of AI in Public Services. Nature Machine Intelligence, 2(1), 6-8.
- Gil-Garcia, J. R., & Pardo, T. A. (2015). Understanding the Role of Government in Smart City Initiatives: An Analysis of the Case Studies of Barcelona, Amsterdam, and Rome. Government Information Quarterly, 32(4), 434-443.
- Gartner. (2021). Innovation Insight for Legacy Modernization by Combining AI, Business Process Management, and Robotic Process Automation. Gartner, Inc.

www.ingramcontent.com/pod-product-compliance
Lightning Source LLC
LaVergne TN
LVHW051329050326
832903LV00031B/3431